Foundational, humbling, and searing – that's how I found this book.

Foundational, because here's the handbook for the Scriptural principles for your work. As a city worker says in the foreword: 'What I would have given to have had the benefit of this book at the outset of my working life.'

Humbling, because John Lennox has actually done two jobs simultaneously over the last fifty years – Oxford academic, and apologist. I wince when I think about how hard he must have laboured, so from personal experience he knows what he's talking about. And lastly, searing, because of the warnings about both idleness and exploitation among those in full-time Christian work.

RICO TICE
Senior Minister (Evangelism), All Souls, Langham Place, London

With a mathematician's precision, Dr Lennox presents an array of business factors that I wish I had read before starting my own company thirty-five years ago. The dividends one will add from reading this will multiply business success exponentially. My word of advice: read this book and take its messages to heart!

MARK LANIER
The Lanier Law Firm, Founder, Lanier Foundation, Houston, Texas

Across the pages of history, great Christian thinkers from the Apostle Paul to Martin Luther and Abraham Kuyper have affirmed the Lordship of Christ over every sphere of life including, crucially, vocation and the workplace. In this book, John Lennox adds to that reservoir of wisdom by affirming defining principles which should shape or reshape our approach to vocation, the workplace, and the creation and management of wealth. This book is dripping with wisdom gleaned both from biblical insights and life experience. It will provide great help, encouragement, and joyful inspiration to all who are seeking to apply the Lordship of Christ in all these vital areas of life.

LINDSAY BROWN
Former General Secretary, International Fellowship of Evangelical Students (IFES), International Director of the Lausanne Movement

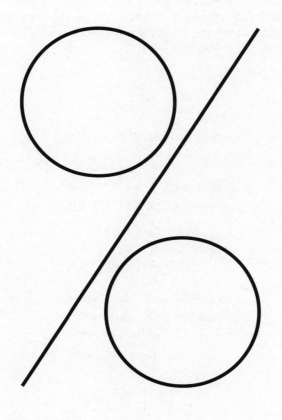

A GOOD RETURN

BIBLICAL PRINCIPLES FOR WORK, WEALTH AND WISDOM

JOHN C. LENNOX

CHRISTIAN
FOCUS

Copyright © John C Lennox 2023

paperback ISBN 978-1-5271-0992-6
ebook ISBN 978-1-5271-1036-6

10 9 8 7 6 5 4 3 2 1

Published in 2023
by
Christian Focus Publications Ltd,
Geanies House, Fearn, Ross-shire,
IV20 1TW, Great Britain.

www.christianfocus.com

Cover design by
Alister MacInnes

Printed and bound by
Bell & Bain, Glasgow

Contents

For Akeel and Joy Sachak with love and gratitude on the occasion of their joint 60th birthdays.

FOREWORD

What I would have given to have had the benefit of this book at the outset of my working life as a banker, rather than today, when I am much closer to the end of my working life: or, at least, the current phase of it. I wonder how I might have done things differently. Instead, I have travelled through most of my working life without clear answers to the questions that John addresses in this book. I have had the privilege of knowing him for many years, and have marvelled at the way in which God has deployed his formidable intellect, his robust biblical understanding, and his talent as a writer, to bring God's teaching from scripture, to speak into many of the questions and issues of our age.

In this book, John has put pen to paper in a uniquely refreshing and stimulating manner on a subject matter that I have long wrestled with as a Christian. Attempts are often made to persuade us that our work lives have little to do with God's plan and purposes, whereas the God-oriented part of our lives is defined by what we do outside of work, despite the fact that we spend the majority of our waking hours at work in body and mind. John brilliantly unravels the wealth of biblical teaching about how we should view our work, and how God sees our work in the context of His overarching creation plan. From that perspective, John methodically, and exhaustively tackles the countless issues and questions with which work confronts us daily, whereas we often make do without answering, or answering with little biblical rigour.

I find it incredibly empowering and heartening to understand that our desire to work, which occupies so much of our lives, is a fundamental aspect of the way God has made us. It makes me think about my work and its purpose, very differently, when I reflect on it being an aspect of being made in the image of God, whose own work is supremely demonstrated in His creation. It also means that, whatever else the New Creation may hold for us, it won't mean the cessation of work, any more than it did before the Fall – and that again changes my perspective on work.

A big area of confusion for me, and no doubt for many Christian workers, who came from a failure to distinguish between the primary purpose, or motivation, with what should be seen as the secondary purpose, or outcome, of our work. John analyses this with his characteristic rigour, and helps us to be clear as a result about why we work, and how to see our work in the context of God's plan for our lives, especially God's call for us to proclaim the gospel.

I had latterly just about figured out that my work was what God had called me to do as my service to Him. However, like many other Christians, I perceived my calling to serve God in a secular workplace to be a second-class ministry by comparison with those called to serve in a church. It is incredibly empowering to discover that there is no biblical basis for this belief. We read countless passages in scripture which can lead us into all sorts of cul-de-sacs. It is like supposing that the Parable of the Rich Fool, or the Parable of the Rich Young Ruler, are to be simplistically understood as biblical exhortations: to give away all our wealth, if we are truly to follow Jesus, or, at the other end of the spectrum, to imagine that if our salvation is by grace alone, through faith alone, then what we do with our money does not have any eternal significance – so we can do with it what we choose.

John also tackles the all-important question of where we invest the wealth which our work generates in order to promote God's glory. This is a theme that has been dear to my own heart for many years. I feel a responsibility to help, indeed, to convince and convict, the current generation of Christians to understand and respond to the challenge of being gospel patrons. God has used Christian patrons throughout church history to partner with and resource those called to proclaim His Word and build His church. To state the obvious, one would not be possible without the other, which transforms the way we can view those called to work to support others in ministry.

I commend this book to anyone and everyone who is engaged in the kind of work where they are tempted to think that what they are doing is a this-world necessity of no eternal consequence. I commend this book to those who think that their work is a consequence of the Fall, and not part of the way God intended us to live. I commend this book to those who think the fruits of their work belong to them, and not to God. I commend this book to those who think their work cannot be part of God's salvation plan for the world. To all these people, this book will be a startling challenge to their current way of thinking about work, wealth and God.

Akeel Sachak
Partner and Global Head of Consumer, Rothschild & Co.

ACKNOWLEDGEMENTS

I would like to thank the many people who have had input into my thinking on this topic over the years including several generations of students who have attended my classes. In particular, I am grateful to Akeel Sachak for writing the Foreword and to Rico Tice, Mark Lanier and Lindsay Brown for their generous endorsements. I am also grateful to Professor David Cranston and to Simon Pillar for valuable comments.

PREFACE

The coronavirus pandemic has caused a radical shake-up in the world of work. Many people who thought their jobs were secure, especially in the hospitality, leisure and travel sectors, have suddenly found themselves without employment, and therefore unable to pay their bills and support their homes and families. Many other people, particularly those in the health and care sectors, have found themselves worked into the ground, and developing all kinds of mental health symptoms under the relentless pressure they are under, to help the desperately ill and dying. The ethos of work has changed with a mass movement to work at home, or to be furloughed for considerable periods of time, with no guarantee of a job to go back to. The pandemic also brought another issue to the fore: the need to rethink the proximity of workers in their workspace, in order to preserve a healthy degree of social distancing.

Not only that, but Russia's invasion of Ukraine has disrupted energy supplies particularly in Western Europe, and the price of energy, fuel and many other things, has skyrocketed with millions struggling for the first time to make ends meet. Fear and uncertainty stalk many homes, as work and income stability have been lost.

Even more, all the time there is the relentless advance of technology, with robotics and artificial intelligence taking over many jobs that were once thought secure – in logistics, transport, manufacturing, marketing, banking, law, medicine, education, and a host of other areas, so that scenarios, not only of unemployment, but also of unemployability, are increasingly being discussed. The jobs most at risk from automation are those that involve routine tasks, such as bookkeeping, secretarial work, and work on the factory floor. Their highly repetitive and predictable activities are nowadays easily programmed into efficient machines that can work 24/7, and do not need to be paid once they have been purchased.[1]

Aristotle saw the problem centuries ago. In 350 BC he wrote:

> 'For if every instrument could accomplish its own work, obeying or anticipating the will of others, like the statues of Daedalus, or the tripods of Hephaestus, which, says the poet, "of their own accord entered the assembly of the Gods"; if, in like manner, the shuttle would weave and the plectrum touch the lyre without a hand to guide them, chief workmen would not want servants, nor masters' slaves.'[2]

In the 2016 film *The Future of Work and Death,* Gray Scott, a futurist and techno-philosopher, said that up to a third of jobs in America could be replaced by robots or automated systems by 2025. Dr Stuart Armstrong of the Future of Humanity Institute added that the least vulnerable are those with people skills and creativity like choreographers, managers and social workers. His study estimated that up to 47 percent of all American jobs could be replaced by 2036.

In light of this, it is not surprising that the topic of the future of work has moved into mainstream academia, as societies wrestle with the task of ensuring employment for their citizens, realising that in certain areas, things will never return to the pre-pandemic state. For instance, according to globally wide-ranging McKinsey Consumer Pulse surveys, around three-quarters of people who used digital channels for the very first time during the pandemic say they will continue to do so if and when things return to some kind of normality. This means that digital skills are at a premium, a

---

[1] For more information on Artificial Intelligence see my *2084: Artificial Intelligence and the Future of Humanity*, (Grand Rapids, Zondervan, 2020).

[2] Aristotle, *Politics*, (London, Penguin 1992), 1:iv.

circumstance that creates difficulty in countries where there is little educational or technical infrastructure to equip people with those skills.

It is far from an easy time for a great number of people. Each worldview has its own approach to work. As such it is important that those of us who espouse the Christian worldview, are acquainted with what it teaches about work, which, above all, is dignified by the fact that God Himself ordained it for human beings to do.

I am acutely aware that there are many books on the biblical perspective on work. Nevertheless, almost every time I have given a talk on these issues, someone has suggested that I should put the material into a book. After long hesitation, I have taken that encouragement to heart. One source of that hesitation is that our work experiences are varied. I have been a university teacher and research mathematician most of my life, with special interest in philosophy and ethics. At the same time, I have been engaged in Bible teaching, in the public defence of the Christian faith, as well as having an active family life. Hence, I think on the plus side that I have some understanding of the pressures of holding together lecturing; research; organisational, pastoral and family commitments – specialised though some of these activities necessarily are.

However, you, the reader, may therefore feel with some justification that I have little direct idea of the sort of work pressures that you may face if you are, say: a farmer, lawyer, surgeon, plumber, builder, accountant, miner, cook, sailor, homemaker, single mum, airline pilot, investment banker, police officer, civil servant – or any one of ten thousand other things that you might be, including unemployed. That said, experience has taught me that the actual issues we face as Christians in the workplace, whether in the home, factory, or office, have a great deal in common. I intend, therefore, to discuss the biblical principles that I have found helpful in my own work, in the hope that you can tweak them to apply to your own situation.

A further motivation for writing has been the fact that over the years I have met all too many Christians who are disappointed that their churches express little or no interest in what they as faithful members do in their workplace – the arena where they may well spend most of their time, whether in their home or outside it. Worse still, some committed churchgoers are made to feel like second-class Christians, trailing behind those who are in so-called 'full-time' Christian work. On the other hand, the fact that salvation is by God's grace, and does not depend on our merit or achievement, may lead yet others to draw the erroneous view that our work is of very little eternal significance.

In a famous lecture entitled *Why Work?* given during the war in 1942, and still well worth reading, Dorothy L. Sayers forcibly addressed the first of these issues:

> 'In nothing has the Church so lost Her hold on reality as in Her failure to understand and respect the secular vocation. She has allowed work and religion to become separate departments, and is astonished to find that, as a result, the secular work of the world is turned to purely selfish and destructive ends, and that the greater part of the world's intelligent workers have become irreligious, or at least, uninterested in religion.'

> 'But is it astonishing? How can anyone remain interested in a religion which seems to have no concern with nine-tenths of his life? The Church's approach to an intelligent carpenter is usually confined to exhorting him not to be drunk and disorderly in his leisure hours, and to come to church on Sundays. What the Church should be telling him is this: that the very first demand that his religion makes upon him is that he should make good tables.'[3]

I wish to encourage such people who have experienced such negativity by showing them that God Himself shows a great deal of interest in our work precisely because it really is of eternal significance. The Bible contains principles that can help us resolve many of the misunderstandings that surround the topic of work, even among Christians.

I imagine that all of us will readily understand the following reaction to a work situation.

---

[3]   https://malyonworkplace.org.au/wp-content/uploads/2013/12/Why-Work-Dorothy-Sayers-Essay.pdf

We Christians say that God is everywhere, and He is Lord of everything but for the majority the honest reality is that our work and marketplaces seem so devoid of God and His purpose. We march off to work valiantly and come home despondently. What is the place and purpose of work? Is there anything sacred about secular work? Is there meaning in the marketplace? Is our great destiny simply to eat, drink and leave behind an empty dish?

That was an honest, heartfelt statement by a Christian living and working in Singapore. It could be echoed by Christians in many parts of the world. We all understand it. 'Just think about it: if you start at 20 and retire at 65 having worked 40 hours a week for 48 weeks a year you will have done nearly 90,000 hours of work. That adds up to just over 10 years of your life.' Is God relevant to any of this, or do we simply have to accept that most of us need to work to live, so that we should simply get on with it?

Many years ago, during the time of the Cold War, I was on the eastern side of the infamous Berlin wall, chatting to young people. One young man expressed his envy of my possession of a passport that allowed me to travel both East and West. Somehow, we got to discussing the Christian faith, and he told me that he was not impressed. He said that communism was clearly far superior to Christianity, in that it was an ideology that had something to say about all of life. It had a philosophy of history, of politics, of literature, of art, of education, and of work. It seemed to him that Christianity, by contrast, occupied very little space and time in a person's life – an hour or so on a Sunday and perhaps, if you were very committed, another hour midweek. 'Your Christianity,' he said, 'is far less than an ideology. It is unimpressive and worthless. Why would anyone take it seriously when it demands so little?'

I have never forgotten him. For, I realised that, when it comes to actual practice, some people professing Christianity give the impression that their faith in God is area-restricted, time-limited, undemanding, and has little or nothing to say about daily life as a whole. What that young East German said to me was, and remains, a challenge to me, and to all Christian believers, to get our act together and wake up to the fact that Christianity, even more than communism, offers us guidance for all aspects of life. In particular, it has much to instruct us about that large expanse of life that is taken up with work.

In her lecture *Why Work?* cited above, Dorothy Sayers, referred to an earlier talk she had given:

> 'What I urged then was a thoroughgoing revolution in our whole attitude to work. I asked that it should be looked upon, not as a necessary drudgery to be undergone for the purpose of making money, but as a way of life in which the nature of man should find its proper exercise and delight, and so fulfil itself to the glory of God.'

This is a thoroughly biblical view. In Genesis we read: 'The Lord God took the man and put him in the garden of Eden to work it and keep it' (Gen. 2:15). The Hebrew term used here for *work* is *avodah*. This is the very same term as is used by Moses: 'Then the Lord said to Moses, "Go in to Pharaoh and say to him, 'Thus says the Lord, "Let my people go, that they may *serve* me"'" (Ex. 8:1). This means that the concepts of work in the ordinary sense and service to God are so closely related in the Hebrew mind that the same word is used for both. The same idea is repeated in the New Testament. Paul writes: 'Whatever you do, *work* heartily, as for the Lord and not for men, knowing that from the Lord you will receive the inheritance as your reward. You are *serving* the Lord Christ' (Col. 3:23-24). Here the word for *serving* is related to the Greek word, *doulos*, for a *slave* or *servant*. It is this close link between God and work that we wish to examine in detail.

I scarcely need to mention that what I have to say will not necessarily enhance your job prospects. Nor will you find the answers to all of your questions and solutions to all of your problems in these pages. When I was younger, like many others, I imagined that I would solve most of life's problems by the age of thirty and then I would begin to live. I explained this to someone older and wiser, who told me that I had it all wrong – wrestling with life's problems, and solving them, is living. I have found that perspective both enlightening and liberating ever since. The Bible is not a manual full of solutions to every conceivable problem that any of us will ever meet. It mainly gives us principles that can shape our lives in developing our character, and helping us mature and become more experienced in tackling life's challenges. I shall, therefore, discuss the biblical teaching on the purpose and meaning of work in the hope of helpfully mapping out a Christian perspective and some principles on how work fits into a bigger, integrated picture of life. I have added an Appendix on biblical principles for the support of the gospel.

We shall see that developing a Christian mind on work is intimately connected with growing a Christian character, and that, in itself, is an attribute that will certainly prove helpful, both in job applications and, of course, in doing the work itself.

The book need not necessarily be read in linear fashion: the reader may go directly to a topic of particular interest and catch up with the rest later.

Questions

1. How have the pandemic and the energy crisis affected your attitude to work?
2. Has the rise of technology made you concerned about your work, or do you think technology will supply a new range of jobs? Would you think of changing your job because of the technology revolution?
3. Is your church interested in what you do during the week? If not, why do you think that is, and what might you do to improve the situation?
4. Do you 'march off to work valiantly and come home despondently'? If so, what might help you mitigate this?
5. Discuss Dorothy Sayers' statement that our 'work should be looked upon – not as a necessary drudgery to be undergone for the purpose of making money, but as a way of life, in which the nature of man should find its proper exercise and delight, and so fulfil itself to the glory of God'.

Summary of Book

Chapter 1
Creation and Sabbath
The first reference to work, in the biblical narrative, is God's original work of creating the heavens and earth, in a sequence of day-stages, followed by rest that become a model for the human workweek. We discuss the work-rest cycle – in particular the meaning and relevance of sabbath in the contemporary world. We conclude by thinking about the status of the sabbath for the Christian, and the importance of the theological doctrine of salvation by faith in Christ, and not by works of personal merit.

Chapter 2
Motivation for Work and Life
In this chapter, we unpack Jesus' main teaching on motivation for work and life that is to be found in His Sermon on the Mount. We start with three key questions: where do we invest; how do we see the world; and which master do we serve? The first and third are about money, the middle one is about perception, and in connection with these we draw on some fascinating recent work on the structure and function of the human brain.

How we answer those questions will affect our levels of anxiety in life in general, and work in particular. Jesus issues a radical command and, in the context of supplying our daily needs, instructs us to seek first God's kingdom and His righteousness, and we shall find that the needs are met. We explore what this means by differentiating, using examples, between the goal of work, and its by-products or outcomes.

Chapter 3
Seeking God's Kingdom in Work
We start the chapter by further exploring the meaning of seeking the kingdom of God in daily work, by studying the experience of Peter's miraculous catch of fish recorded in Luke 5. We then move on to what the Bible has to say about morality, money, power, and sex in the workplace. We look in particular

at the examples of Joseph and Nehemiah to highlight the
pressures that work can put upon us.

Chapter 4
Secular or Sacred?
The account of Peter's transition, in the previous chapter, from
a fisherman to a fisher of men and women, now leads us to
look at the widespread notion that there are two classes of
Christians: those who earn their keep in secular employment,
and those who are employed full-time by the church – and that
the latter are superior to the former. We therefore investigate
this whole idea and find it to be erroneous and unhelpful by
contrast with the biblical idea of work as calling.

Chapter 5
Gospel Patrons
From the very beginning, the progress of the gospel in
the world has depended in large part on the generosity of
believers. Jesus and His disciples were supported in their
itinerant ministry by a group of women believers, and Paul's
mission to Europe was facilitated by a businesswoman, Lydia.
Throughout the centuries, gospel patronage, by both wealthy
and poor Christians, has been practised as a Christian grace
of giving. We give examples of this and look at some of the
principles involved.

However, there are different kinds of wealth, even more
important than monetary wealth – think of Paul's intellectual
and spiritual wealth. We look at the way in which various
kinds of wealth have been brought together to maintain the
momentum of the gospel.

Chapter 6
Wealth Management
Although there are many different kinds of wealth, the Bible
nevertheless has a great deal to say about how believers are
to relate to material wealth. Jesus Himself taught about it in
a number of memorable parables that we discuss in order to
discover the principles that they illustrate: the rich fool, the
lost son, the dishonest steward, and the rich man and Lazarus.

We conclude the chapter by looking at the encounter between Jesus and Zacchaeus, the tax collector.

Chapter 7
Eternal Rewards
Jesus constantly emphasised that there is a connection between what we do in this life, and our experience in the world to come. Though entrance to heaven cannot be merited by our work, both Jesus and His apostles taught that there are to be rewards of various kinds, not only for the work we have done for the Lord, but also in connection with the character we have developed. We look at the principles that will operate at what is called the judgement seat of Christ, and spell out its implications for the way in which we order our lives on earth.

Appendix A
Principles of Gospel Support
In this section we examine in more detail the biblical principles governing the support of the gospel – principles for both giver and recipient.

Appendix B
Insights from Neuroscience
Here we develop further the important ideas of Iain McGilchrist, outlined in Chapter 2, on the functioning of the two cerebral hemispheres that constitute the human brain.

CHAPTER 1

CREATION AND SABBATH

Work was God's idea. Genesis tells us how it all started. The first thing it teaches us about God, fundamental to the whole biblical narrative, is that God is a worker who both created and ordered the world, and that He did it in such a way to provide us with the universally familiar pattern of a working week – six days of activity, followed by a day of rest.[1]

On the sixth day, we are told, God reached the pinnacle of His creative activity by making human beings, men and women, in His own image. The importance of this fact cannot possibly be over-emphasised. For instance, Canadian intellectual and psychologist Jordan Peterson, says that this Genesis statement about humans being created in the image of God is foundational for Western civilization and values. From it he deduces that: 'Each individual has something of transcendent value about them... I tell you, we dispense with that idea at our serious peril.'[2]

---

[1] For a detailed discussion of how to understand the Genesis 1 text see my: *Seven Days that Divide the World*, 10th Anniversary Edition, (Grand Rapids, Zondervan 2021).

[2] From a 2nd Lecture on Genesis.

'The heavens declare the glory of God,' says Psalm 19:1. Every time I look at the Orion Nebula or the Andromeda Galaxy through my telescope my mind is filled with awe at their sheer magnificence. Yet, the heavens, though glorious, were not made in God's image. We humans were, and that gives us incalculable dignity and value.

God's work was to create and order the world, and we who are made in His image are privileged to be creators, albeit in a much lesser sense. This is true of all of us – whether we are a factory worker, farmer, teacher, artist, musician, cleaner, homemaker. We get a sense of accomplishment by making and organising things.

God placed the first humans in a garden (Eden) and instructed them to tend and keep it. The first human work, then, that we read about, was gardening. We note in passing that this work was, for obvious reasons, unpaid and it will be important for us not to fall into the trap of imagining that the only kind of work that matters is paid work. In fact, much work today is unpaid: the care of families and relatives, and all kinds of voluntary work, either individual or organised at home, church and elsewhere, without which many an economy would collapse.

We also learn that the first humans' environment had the potential for realising many different kinds of work. Aside from the fruit and crops produced by gardening, we read that there were four rivers that watered the garden, and Genesis 2 intriguingly describes what you would find if you followed their courses. One, for instance, led to a region where there was mineral wealth – gold, indeed, good quality gold, could be found there. That serves to remind us of human curiosity and the vast areas of work that the desire to know about the world has opened up – exploration, mining, mineral working and research and development of all kinds. Humans are curious beings, and that curiosity fuels employment for millions. After all, I got paid for research in pure mathematics! However, there is justification for that because so many disciplines rely on mathematics.

Genesis tells us that Adam was not only given the physical agricultural work of cultivating the garden, he was also tasked with the abstract intellectual activity of naming the animals. Assigning names to things, or to give it its more sophisticated title, taxonomy, is a fundamental academic discipline. 'Naming is taming,' says the old phrase, and no matter how simple or profound our activity, from plumbing to aircraft manufacture, from knitting to nuclear physics, we have to learn the vocabulary appropriate to that activity. I know the vocabulary of mathematics but not the vocabulary of car mechanics or knitting, apart from a word or two!

As humans proliferated, all kinds of new activities developed as, relying on each other's skills, they learned to trade with each other. It was the foundation of economic interdependence on which civilised societies depend.

Genesis teaches us that God gave humans the honour and dignity of being stewards of His creation. They were not granted licence to exploit creation and thus to destroy the delicate balance of its ecosystem with no thought of what they were doing. They were to maintain and care for it (and themselves) responsibly as the Creator's viceroys. That ongoing task is currently of paramount importance as global warming and climate change threaten to engulf the planet in multiple catastrophes. God is far from being indifferent to the way in which we treat the planet. In Revelation John describes the reaction of the twenty-four elders to God's taking over the reins of government:

> Then the seventh angel blew his trumpet, and there were loud voices in heaven, saying, 'The kingdom of the world has become the kingdom of our Lord and of his Christ, and he shall reign forever and ever.' And the twenty-four elders who sit on their thrones before God fell on their faces and worshipped God, saying,
>
> 'We give thanks to you, Lord God Almighty,
>   who is and who was,
> for you have taken your great power
>   and begun to reign.
> The nations raged,
>   but your wrath came,
>   and the time for the dead to be judged,
> and for rewarding your servants, the prophets and saints,

and those who fear your name,
both small and great,
and for destroying the destroyers of the earth.' (11:15-18)

The final phrase shows exactly what God thinks of those who lay waste the earth.

That original situation in Eden sounds idyllic. It is sometimes referred to as *paradise,* a word derived via French, Latin and Greek from an old Iranian term meaning *a park enclosed by a wall.*

Yet, a great deal of work nowadays is far from idyllic: some of it is repetitive drudgery, some is very risky to life and limb, some is horrifically exploitative involving inadequate pay, child labour and even slavery, that are a blemish on humanity. There are thorns and thistles in both a literal and a metaphorical sense to be found everywhere. There is serious moral evil in many work environments.

Genesis tells us that this circumstance results from a horrific disaster that wrecked the paradise of Eden when moral evil, that is, sin, entered the world through human disobedience to the word of God. That event, often called the Fall, has self-evidently affected us all. In particular, it has turned work into toil and introduced thorns and thistles, both literal and metaphorical, into every aspect of the world. It also led to human physical death.

As a result, work of any kind may often become frustrating, unsatisfying, stressful, boring, disappointing, and full of tricky relationships and moral problems. The litany of woe is endless. We are damaged workers living in a damaged world. Indeed, in New Testament times, many believers were slaves in Roman households and had to endure all the unfairness and pain of that status; many others were crushed and exploited under ruthless tax regimes, of which, as we shall see, Paul was well aware.

That is not to say that work can never bring any joy, satisfaction, or sense of fulfilment. Far from it. But it is clear from the start that there is no guarantee that we shall have job satisfaction, even if we are believers in God. Nevertheless, even after the Fall, work remains important in that *it* itself is not a consequence of the Fall, as some erroneously imagine.

No, work is an integral part of God's creation ordinance helping shape what it means to be human, and therefore, Paul encourages us: 'Whatever you do, work heartily, as for the Lord and not for men.' (Col. 3:23)

We are moving too fast. For, as part of the creation cycle, God established a further institution:

THE SABBATH: THE WORK-REST CYCLE

The book of Genesis depicts God as a worker, fashioning the creation in six periods of activity followed by a seventh day of rest.[3] This creation pattern established the cycle of work and rest for human beings and, therefore, in any consideration of work, it is important to think about the necessity of taking regular rest from that work.

Built into human nature is the need for physical and psychological rest in the form of sleep every twenty-four hours. According to the *Theology of Work Project*, a survey by the American Psychological Association showed that more than a third of workers experience chronic work stress, which can lead to anxiety, insomnia, muscle pain, increased blood pressure, as well as a weakened immune system. This kind of stress can also increase chances of heart disease, diabetes, and depression. Furthermore, exhaustion depletes a person's skill at managing interpersonal relationships. Studies show that, when someone is tired, he or she misreads other people's social signals. A tired person is more prone to project negative motives onto other people and will find it hard to resist lashing out in response. Irritability and a short fuse are classic symptoms of an urgent need to rest and recuperate. Finally, lack of rest has spiritual implications. God created both work and rest, and carelessness in these areas can estrange people from Him.

We need our sleep, certainly, but we need more than sleep. The Bible insisted on one full day's rest in seven, a regulation which became the Sabbath law that was part of the covenant between God and Israel, laid down in Exodus 20:8-11. And

---

[3]   The reader interested in pursuing the matter of the Genesis sequence of days is referred to my book, *Seven Days that Divide the World*, 10th Anniversary Edition, (Grand Rapids, Zondervan 2021).

many of us will testify that rest time can be creative time. Famous scientists tell us that some of their best ideas occur when they are not officially at work, but out for a walk, crossing a road, or even dozing by a fire.

The importance of the Sabbath is to be seen particularly in light of idolatry.

The danger of work becoming an idol

Work of whatever kind can take over our lives, and become an all-consuming idol that takes precedence even over God Himself. It is like an intoxicating drink – we speak of people whose work is so all-consuming, becoming workaholics who run the risk of burn out and mental breakdown. This can happen to anyone – Christian or otherwise – and one of its first signs is exhaustion. The other two are cynicism and ineffectiveness. How easily that happens – we get to work early and stay late. We bring piles of work home, carry on through hasty meals with smartphones glued to our ears and laptops to our fingers and eyes; to send just one more email to clinch that next deal, to outsell our competitors, or to climb that next rung on the ladder. In the meantime, neglected family life is burned up on the altar of our idolatrous attachment to work. That is what making work an idol can do to us – the idol sucks the life out of us, even as we seek to find our meaning in it. We become cynical since, like the pagan idols of old, work has become a crushing weight that has to be carried. God, by contrast, if we let Him, is prepared to carry us and make us effective again.

Yet burn out is not always the result of making an idol of our work. Some people are put under relentless pressure by others until the burden becomes intolerable. A Barna Study has revealed that such was the case in 2021: 38 percent considered giving up their ministry. One such pastor reports that constant, wearing discussion about issues that surrounded the pandemic has left him feeling, 'as if everyone is on a hair-trigger, ready to walk away at the merest hint that the church does not line up with their political, or personal perspectives'.[4]

---

[5] Report by Peter Chin, in *Christianity Today*, February 2, 2022.

This pastor found his main relief in the beautiful restfulness of the Hebrew concept of *chesed* (loving kindness).

Hence the enduring importance of the sabbath, whose main reason was to remind us that we need regular rest in order to recalibrate and recuperate. From time to time, Jesus called His disciples to 'Come away ... and rest a while' (Mark 6:31). We neglect this at our peril. Former UK Chief Rabbi Jonathan Sacks writes of the Sabbath, 'It is a day that sets a limit to our intervention in nature and to our economic activity. We become conscious of being creations, not creators. The earth is not ours, but God's. The Sabbath is a weekly reminder of the integrity of nature and the boundaries of human striving.' His statement recalls a memorable phrase of Os Guinness : 'The modern world has scrambled things so badly that today we worship our work, we work at our play, and we play at our worship.'[5] That is, the sabbath reminds us that we regularly need to make a conscious effort to see our lives in a bigger context than that of our daily work.

If you recognise yourself as failing in this respect, there is only one thing to do: stop and rest! A well-known British evangelist once ruefully commented, 'I didn't take a day off and had a breakdown and then all the days I missed I took in a row.' Two well-known British evangelists, John Chapman and Rico Tice were chatting. Rico said, 'I often don't take a day off. I don't have time.' Chapo responded, 'If we break God's laws, they will break us.'[6]

Much overwork is driven by fear: fear of being left behind, of not putting on a good show, of letting the company down, of letting the bottomline slip. In short, fear of failure and rejection. That acts like a slave-driver's whip to wind us up to even more effort and more exhaustion. That is why we need to think about a second reason for the Sabbath, that is given to us in Deuteronomy 5:15: 'You shall remember that you were a slave in the land of Egypt, and the Lord your God brought you out from there with a mighty hand and an outstretched arm. Therefore, the Lord your God commanded you to keep the Sabbath day.' The Sabbath was intended as a day of rest during

---

[5] Os Guinness, *The Call: Finding and Fulfilling the Central Purpose of Your Life.*

[6] Inserted with Rico Tice's permission.

which Israel had opportunity to remember that they had been redeemed by God from the slave labour camps in Egypt – a time when they had been forced to work impossible hours without any rest. It is a sad tragedy today when Christians force themselves, or are forced by unconscionable employers, to slave away for impossible hours without rest. They, or their employers, have forgotten both creation and redemption – that is, they have forgotten that work needs to be seen in a larger context.

If we are workaholics, forcing ourselves to overwork, then we need to rest and think about the fact that we have been redeemed.

Sadly, the concept of a day of rest has been severely eroded in many countries, as increasing commercial pressures permit less recreation and family time for many people.

Concern about the status of the Sabbath arose in New Testament times, especially in churches where there was a mixed community of Jewish and Gentile believers. Sabbath-keeping threatened to become an issue, since it was mandatory for Jews, and non-Jews knew nothing of it, except in so far as they had observed the Jewish practices of their neighbours.

What was the Christian attitude to the Sabbath to be? Must it be Sunday? Surely not, since on Sundays, ministers and pastors are usually engaged with church services and so they often take Monday as their day of rest. Sunday, for the Christian, is described in the New Testament as *the Lord's Day*, the day of Jesus' resurrection. This has nothing to do either with work or the Sabbath: indeed, the Lord's Supper may have been so-called because it was held in the evening after a day's work! In this connection, we note that the Jewish Sabbath was, and still is, Saturday.

There is no injunction in Scripture saying either that Saturday is the Sabbath for Christians, as Seventh Day Adventists claim, or that Sunday is now to be regarded as the Sabbath, as claimed by some of Sabbatarian persuasion who transfer the prohibition of work for Jews on Saturday and apply it to Christians on Sunday.

In order to understand this matter of sabbath-keeping we need to look at the teaching of Jesus Himself. He prepared the way for a new understanding in the Gospels by His reaction to accusations of breaking the Sabbath, for instance, in allowing His disciples to rub grains of corn to eat in Matthew 12:1-8, and in healing the man born blind, in John 9.

In the former incident, Jesus strongly defended His disciples' action. They were, He pointed out, engaged in His service which was – in the fullest possible sense – the service of God. He then cited an Old Testament precedent: 'The priests in the temple break the Sabbath and are guiltless.' He went on to add: 'The Son of Man is Lord of the Sabbath.' This tells us that the Sabbath, though part of God's covenant with Israel, and therefore obligatory for Israel, is not a moral law. For, by very definition of the words 'moral' and 'guilt', you cannot break a moral law and be guiltless. This becomes obvious if you try to replace Sabbath in Jesus' statement by any of the moral laws contained in the ten commandments – for example, to say that the priests in the temple steal, or commit adultery, etc., and are guiltless, would be morally absurd.

Incidentally, that is why we find all of the moral commandments repeated in the New Testament as norms for Christian behaviour. The Sabbath law, by contrast, is not a moral commandment, and hence treatment of it in the New Testament is in different terms.

Paul, towards the end of his letter to the church at Rome, which had members that had been converted to Christianity from both Jewish and Gentile backgrounds, lays down guidelines for regulating differences of opinion on matters of conscience over food, and the observance of days:

> As for the one who is weak in faith, welcome him, but not to quarrel over opinions. One person believes he may eat anything, while the weak person eats only vegetables. Let not the one who eats despise the one who abstains and let not the one who abstains pass judgement on the one who eats, for God has welcomed him. Who are you to pass judgement on the servant of another? It is before his own master that he stands or falls. And he will be upheld, for the Lord is able to make him stand.
>
> One person esteems one day as better than another, while another esteems all days alike. Each one should be fully

convinced in his own mind. The one who observes the day, observes it in honour of the Lord. The one who eats, eats in honour of the Lord, since he gives thanks to God, while the one who abstains, abstains in honour of the Lord and gives thanks to God. For none of us lives to himself, and none of us dies to himself. For if we live, we live to the Lord, and if we die, we die to the Lord. So then, whether we live or whether we die, we are the Lord's. For to this end Christ died and lived again, that he might be Lord both of the dead and of the living. (Rom. 14:1-9)

Paul is writing here about matters of conscience, not moral issues, and regulating the situation in the interest of promoting harmony among believers of differing convictions. The important thing for Paul was that believers did not sit in judgement on each other when they differed in their practice, where no moral principle was involved. Some believers from a Jewish background would still conscientiously observe the Sabbath and refuse to eat pork, whereas others, not having the same conscience, would eat pork and not observe the Sabbath.

Whatever they did, they were to do it unto the Lord. However, Paul was open with them in describing the former group as weak in their consciences and the latter as strong. He was hinting at the fact that their consciences might adjust when they realized that the situation had changed from Old Testament times to New. For Christ had made 'all foods clean' in Mark 7:19, as Peter had had to learn in Acts 10. As a result, the situation now was that each person should be 'fully persuaded in their own mind' as to what they did.

That adjustment of conscience might take some time and so, since living a godly life pleasing to the Lord did not consist in what a person ate or drank (Rom. 14:17), they should not cause any of their fellow believers to stumble, by forcing them to do what they still had a conscience about. As a contemporary example, if I were to invite Jewish or Muslim friends for a meal, in order to avoid offending them, I would not set pork on the table, even though I am personally happy to eat pork, or refrain from it as I wish. My own father, a Christian, had, for a time, a conscience about eating pork. Yet, like Peter, he changed.

There is a further point that needs to be made. Consider the following scenarios.

Scenario 1. Suppose that I have been invited to preach in a church with strong Sabbatarian convictions that extend to forbidding driving on a Sunday.[7] If I insist that I am free in Christ to drive on Sundays, and turn up at this church in a car, I may find that the congregation disappears in protest. So, as no moral principle is involved, I wouldn't do that. Since I wish to be free to preach the gospel, I take Paul's advice and, for the sake of *their* conscience, 'to the Jews I become as a Jew'.

Scenario 2. Now suppose I am a missionary in some remote community. I hear that another missionary would like to visit me. Delighted at the possibility of fellowship with another colleague, I invite him to preach in our small but growing church. At first all goes well. Then, without warning, he tells the congregation that, in order to be saved, a person has to keep the Sabbath. He did not inform me in advance of his strong Sabbatarian convictions.

In this situation, I would not say that he is right to say this, as it is merely a matter of his conscience. No, I would be obliged to intervene and point out that his preaching contradicted the gospel. That is, what was only a matter of conscience in Scenario 1, has now become a serious doctrinal issue in Scenario 2. For the man is teaching that salvation has to be earned, in this case, by Sabbath-keeping. For the sake of the gospel, his view cannot therefore be allowed to stand unchallenged, as it contradicts what the gospel teaches on the relationship of work to salvation.

Many people find it very difficult to grasp this gospel principle, that salvation does not depend on our work or merit. For, work, and particularly paid work, is inextricably connected in most of our minds with merit. We expect to be paid in line with what we do. We expect to be treated by our employers according to our merit and, if we work hard, we expect our relationship with colleagues and employers to be good.

This connection between work and reward is so deep seated that it is easy for us to imagine that it is essentially how

---

[7]   Such churches, though rare, still exist.

the world works in every sphere. One obvious consequence is the widespread yet false idea that religion in general, and Christianity in particular, teaches that God's attitude to us also depends on our work. If we have both been good and done good, we hope eventually to be accepted at the final judgment, and if we have done evil ... well, we don't want to think about that.

THE GROUNDS AND THE FRUIT OF SALVATION

However, God's acceptance and salvation cannot be obtained by our merit, not even by keeping the Sabbath, or doing any number of good works. The good news is that we receive the gift of salvation by trusting in the merit and work of the Lord Jesus Christ, who died on the cross to pay the penalty of our sins. Salvation, as Paul explains, is a gift of God that we cannot earn, but it has to be received:

> For by grace you have been saved through faith. And this is not your own doing; it is the gift of God, not a result of works, so that no one may boast. For we are his workmanship, created in Christ Jesus for good works, which God prepared beforehand, that we should walk in them. (Eph. 2:8-10)

There is, therefore, a sad irony in Scenario 2 above. Making Sabbath-keeping a good work that contributes to salvation is really an oxymoron in that it contradicts the deeper meaning of what Sabbath itself stands for. We saw earlier that the law of Sabbath is not *applied* in its primary sense to believers in the New Testament. True, but it is *interpreted* for believers in Hebrews 4. The writer cites the Sabbath passage from Genesis 1 and, after a lengthy discussion of the nature of rest, concludes by saying, 'There remains a Sabbath rest for the people of God, for whoever has entered God's rest has also rested from his works as God did from his.' (Heb. 4:9-10)

The Genesis account tells us that God rested on the seventh day. He did the work of creating, and then rested from it. We, therefore, inherit a universe that we did not create, merit, or earn. We rest in, receive, and enjoy the fruit of what God has done. The passage now teaches that entering God's spiritual rest, that is, receiving His forgiveness, salvation, and peace, proceeds in an analogous way. Just as God did the work of creation without our help, so, again without our help, God has completed the work of creating a means to redeem us, through the death of Christ for our sins on the cross, and through His resurrection. Therefore, in order to enter into God's rest, we must rest on the work that Christ has done, and *not* on the work we do. Paul makes this principle crystal clear: 'Now to the one who works, his wages are not counted as a gift but as his due. And to the one who does not work but trusts him who justifies the ungodly, his faith is counted as righteousness.' (Rom. 4:4-5)

Paul then goes on to say that we who have received salvation as a gift by putting our faith in Christ are created in Him 'for good works, which God prepared beforehand that we should walk in them'. That is, good works are not the *basis* of salvation, but they are the *fruit* of salvation. God Himself is concerned to see that we produce this fruit.

These principles are important since Christians are prone either:

1. to falling back into imagining that they have to earn God's love, even by their 'Christian work'. This has the effect of producing a joyless, depressing, burdensome existence – a real slavery that can lead to exhaustion. This shows that they have not understood the meaning of Sabbath *rest*;

2. to slip into imagining that because God's salvation is a free gift, He doesn't take their 'lapses' seriously and, in the end, it doesn't really matter how they live. This shows that they have not understood the nature of *redemption*.

If we are busy people, indeed, especially if we are busy people, we need to remind ourselves constantly that we *should* do what we do to please the Lord, because He *has* accepted us. We are not doing it to impress Him, so that He *will* accept us. Only then, will we have the right attitude to our work.

Now there is much more to it than this. Working for the Lord is connected in Scripture with reward. We reserve that topic for later.

Questions

1. Discuss what it means to you that you are made in the image of God? How does that relate to your work and how you do it?
2. Do you think that 'create and order' is a fair summary of what we do? Give examples to illustrate your answer and compare with those of others.
3. What does it mean to be a steward of creation?
4. What was the effect on work of the entry of sin into the world? Can you see evidence of that in your own work?
5. What does sabbath mean to you? How do you practice rest and recuperation?
6. 'If we break God's laws, they will break us.' Discuss – have you personally experienced this?
7. If salvation is by God's grace without works, why should we bother about how we work?

CHAPTER 2

MOTIVATION

A survey in Germany by Focus Magazine asked: what is the most important motivation for work? For nearly half the surveyed group, it was money; for less than half, it was job satisfaction; and for around a fifth, it was collegiality and friendship.

Is God relevant here, or are there just some fortunate people who always seem to get the best jobs, enjoy them to the full, and then there is the rest of us whose moments of joy and job satisfaction are few and far-between, and we simply have to live with that?

None of these questions is easy to answer, and it would be arrogant of me to imagine I could come up with solutions for other people. Of course, I can't. For each of us is a human being, with an inbuilt desire to flourish, and with very different ideas of what that might mean.

Asking the question as to why we work may seem rather foolish, since we might well think that the answer is obvious. Most of us need to work, in order to provide the basic needs of food, clothing, and housing for ourselves, and our dependents.

From both an intuitive and a biblical perspective, the norm is that we should work to provide these things. For instance, some of the proverbs of Solomon, written in the context of a mainly agricultural society, make this clear: 'Whoever works his land will have plenty of bread, but he who follows worthless pursuits lacks sense' (Prov. 12:11). Or: 'The hand of the diligent will rule, while the slothful will be put to forced labour' (Prov. 12:24). Also: 'In all toil there is profit, but mere talk tends only to poverty' (Prov. 14:23).

We get the point; although it is important to say that, according to Scripture, laziness is not the only source of poverty; injustice and oppression are also prime causes: 'The fallow ground of the poor would yield much food, but it is swept away through injustice' (Prov. 13:23).

Paul writes to Christians in Thessalonica about the danger of laziness: 'We urge you brothers to ... aspire to live quietly, and to mind your own affairs, and to work with your hands, as we instructed you, so that you may walk properly before outsiders and be dependent on no one' (1 Thess. 4.10-12). He bluntly reminds them: 'For even when we were with you, we would give you this command: If anyone is not willing to work, let him not eat' (2 Thess. 3:10).

Paul also tells Timothy to make sure he informs the Christians in Ephesus that: '...if anyone does not provide for his relatives, and especially for members of his household, he has denied the faith and is worse than an unbeliever' (1 Tim. 5:8).

Christians are not to be lazy and idle; they are to work to provide for themselves and dependents. One would presume that by dependents are meant those people incapable of providing for themselves. Failing to provide contradicts their professed faith in Christ. On the other hand, it is important that there is real need for help and not simply a dependence based on laziness which exploits generosity. It is not wrong to be discerning – indeed, we are required to be.

Also, there can be serious misunderstanding in another direction. One sad example of this is what has occasionally happened when Christians have applied to themselves Jesus' challenge to the rich young ruler, to sell all that he had and distribute it to the poor (cf. Matt 19:21; Luke 18:22). Leaving themselves and their families nothing to live on, non-Christian relatives have had to step in and help, with the predictable result that they are completely turned off Christianity. We shall look at Jesus' words to the young ruler in more detail later.

Unemployment

We should now notice how carefully Paul expresses himself in the quote above: 'If anyone *will not* work, neither let him eat.' It is easy to get this wrong, as did one Prime Minister (she shall remain nameless!) in misquoting it on one occasion as follows: 'If anyone *does not* work, neither let him eat.' There is a great difference between *will not* and *does not*. There are, sad to say, many people around the world who would love to have a job; they are more than willing to work, but they cannot find employment. To suggest that they should not have food to eat, because they do not have work, is very hurtful; indeed, cruel.

Joblessness can be very distressing. I well recall my teenage son coming home in tears, after yet another job rejection, saying: 'Dad, they didn't *want* me.' That was tough, since God has made work part of what it (normally) means to be human, as we saw from Genesis. So, when we cannot get a job, it is very easy to feel devalued and unwanted. Those of us who have jobs, need to be very thankful for them, and to be sympathetic and understanding towards those people who have difficulties getting employment.

We ought also to be very thankful for those of our number, and indeed, anyone who creates employment for others. As a lifelong teacher and researcher, I have helped train many teachers, and therefore created employment opportunities for them, but I have given direct employment to very few. I greatly respect and admire those who do. We need to encourage the entrepreneurs among us who not only create work for themselves but for others as well, so that their employees can go to bed at night, thankful for what someone else has done for them, that they did not have the ability to do for themselves.

MOTIVATION FOR WORK

We now come to the all-important question of motivation. It is not always easy for us to discover what our own motivation really is. One way that is sometimes helpful is to ask ourselves what our dreams are – and our nightmares. Our hopes and fears can reveal a great deal about what is really driving us. And one of those things is our values. Jesus Himself tells us to think hard about this matter, in His famous Sermon on the Mount:

> 'Do not lay up for yourselves treasures on earth, where moth and rust destroy and where thieves break in and steal, but lay up for yourselves treasures in heaven, where neither moth nor rust destroys and where thieves do not break in and steal. For where your treasure is, there your heart will be also.

> 'The eye is the lamp of the body. So, if your eye is healthy, your whole body will be full of light, but if your eye is bad, your whole body will be full of darkness. If then the light in you is darkness, how great is the darkness!

> 'No one can serve two masters, for either he will hate the one and love the other, or he will be devoted to the one and despise the other. You cannot serve God and money.' (Matt. 6:19-24)

There are three sets of pairs here: two worlds in which one can invest, earth and heaven; two conditions of the eye as an organ of perception, healthy – the word means *single* – and bad; and two masters that one can choose to serve – God and money. These alternatives raise three questions: where do we invest; how do we see the world; and which master do we serve? We look at them briefly here – they will crop up from time to time throughout the book.

1. Where do we invest?

Jesus starts by reminding His audience that this apparently solid world beneath our feet is not the only world in existence. Earth is real, but so is heaven. One of the central claims that Jesus made was that He came down from heaven to earth. Our attitude to work will very much depend on whether we believe in one world or in two. Not everyone has money to invest, but we all have time, energy, and emotional capital, in terms of love, care and commitment, that we can, indeed *must* invest. For instance, we all have only so much time, and we cannot keep it in a box and save it; we have, as we say, to *spend* time. Hence the question is: what do we spend it on? The immediate answer is: on things that we value that the Lord Jesus calls treasure. He tells us that it is possible for us to lay up treasure for ourselves in one of two worlds. What that involves we shall see later on.

2. How do we see?

Jesus has in view not only the physical organ of vision, the eye, but the mind's eye, the gateway to perception. A healthy physical eye will yield clear vision, whereas a diseased eye will distort what is seen, and deliver an imperfect picture of reality. Changing the imagery a little, the world looks physically different through variously tinted spectacles, and at the deeper level the mind perceives the world differently, according to what mental tinted glasses we adopt – in other words, according to our world-view. For instance, the world looks very different to Christian eyes than to atheist eyes. Although the world is really objectively there, nevertheless there is a sense in which the health of our vision, how we pay attention, modifies the world that we see.

Insights from neuroscience can help us here. How we pay attention to the world is the subject matter of a recent magisterial work in two massive volumes, by neuroscientist and polymath Iain McGilchrist. It is called *The Matter with Things: Our Brains, Our Delusions and the Unmaking of the World*.[1]

McGilchrist introduced his basic thesis in 2009 in his fascinating, highly recommended book, *The Master and his Emissary*,[2] written twelve years earlier.

His books focus on the two-hemisphere structure of the human brain. Meticulous research shows that, although the left and right cerebral hemispheres work in concert, and are both involved in virtually all brain activity, each needing the other, there are nevertheless important differences between

---

[1]   London, Perspectiva Press, 2021.

[2]   New Haven, Yale University Press, 2009.

them that have radical implications for our perception of reality.[3] There is an asymmetry between them, two with the left hemisphere emphasising apprehension, and the right comprehension, so that each of them pays attention to the world in a different way, and therefore gives rise to a different kind of knowledge. The left hemisphere helps us manipulate the world; the right helps us understand it. The left is good at categorising and analysing; the right is good at helping us form relationships with others. The left knows things as impersonal objects. The right knows people as persons and as subjects. The left gives us a small fine-grained picture, the right provides a big picture.

A good example of this is to think of a small bird picking up seeds. It is watching the seeds on the ground with its right eye (controlled by the left hemisphere), whilst it is keeping a watch with its left eye (controlled by the right hemisphere), to see the bigger picture of its surroundings where there might lurk a predator raptor.

Much of the work we humans do, especially, but not only, of a repetitive, mechanical kind, is a left-hemisphere activity, whereas creating a bigger context is a right-hemisphere activity. We need both.

Jesus' teaching about good and bad eyes fits perfectly into this understanding of the brain, especially in light of McGilchrist's comments on what happens when the left hemisphere is allowed to dominate: 'The tendency of the left hemisphere is to narrow focus so drastically, that it fails to see the broad picture at all. Therefore it cannot detect that anything is missing when its impoverished picture becomes a supposed representation of the whole.'[4] That is one clear source of a bad eye that fills the mind with darkness.

---

[3]   A helpful presentation of his views is to be found at https://www.youtube.com/watch?v=U99dQrZdVTg

[4]   We shall refer to McGilchrist's work from time to time, in this book and I leave it to the interested reader to discover other places where his insights might usefully be applied. In any case, more information on this topic will be found in Appendix B.

3. Which master do we serve?

The potential masters envisaged by Jesus are God and money.[5] We should notice that we can serve God and use money – a topic that we shall treat in detail in later chapters. What is impossible is to serve God and money together. There is also the further danger that we attempt to serve money, and use God, if and when any trouble arises – a recipe for failure and possible disaster.

The two masters in Jesus' teaching reminds me of McGilchrist's earlier work mentioned above, which can lead to another application of Jesus' teaching, in a different direction. In his book, *The Master and his Emissary*, McGilchrist uses a story by Nietzsche that tells of a king, the master, who rules over a large territory that becomes unmanageable for him. He therefore sends out a competent emissary to represent him. However, the emissary sees an opportunity to outmanoeuver the master, by ingratiating himself with the people, and usurping the master's throne, which he successfully does. McGilchrist uses this as a parable, with the master as the right cerebral hemisphere and the emissary as the left, to warn us of the danger of allowing the left hemisphere to dominate our lives, so that they lose all their value and meaning. This is precisely what will happen if we allow money to dominate our lives. However, in the case of the cerebral hemispheres, we need both of them: It is not one or the other, but a question of which one is permitted to dominate.

We note that two of Jesus' three statements are about money, and the third, His teaching about perception, is sandwiched between them. That circumstance may well indicate that Jesus wishes us to think about perception, particularly in connection with money. A healthy eye directed by the right hemisphere will consider treasure in heaven far more valuable than treasure on earth; a healthy eye will allow the right hemisphere to dominate, and will delightedly and unreservedly serve God rather than money. Giving will be the best antidote to materialism.

The three statements now lead us into Jesus' teaching about anxiety:

---

[5] 'Mammon' is an Aramaic word for money

Therefore, I tell you, do not be anxious about your life, what you will eat or what you will drink, nor about your body, what you will put on. Is not life more than food, and the body more than clothing? Look at the birds of the air: they neither sow nor reap nor gather into barns, and yet your heavenly Father feeds them. Are you not of more value than they? And which of you by being anxious can add a single hour to his span of life? And why are you anxious about clothing? Consider the lilies of the field, how they grow: they neither toil nor spin, yet I tell you, even Solomon in all his glory was not arrayed like one of these.

But if God so clothes the grass of the field, which today is alive and tomorrow is thrown into the oven, will he not much more clothe you, O you of little faith? Therefore, do not be anxious, saying, 'What shall we eat?' or 'What shall we drink?' or 'What shall we wear?' For the Gentiles seek after all these things, and your heavenly Father knows that you need them all. But seek first the kingdom of God and his righteousness, and all these things will be added to you. 'Therefore, do not be anxious about tomorrow, for tomorrow will be anxious for itself. Sufficient for the day is its own trouble.' (Matt. 6:25-34)

The topic of anxiety strikes a chord with many of us. We note that Jesus talks about it in the context of money, food, drink, clothing, and housing, precisely the things that ordinarily motivate people to work. Obtaining them, or enough of them, and ensuring an ongoing supply, is one of life's major sources of concern that can easily lead to anxiety, despair, and even family breakdown, even if we have a job.

Jesus' treatment of anxiety in the context of perception is striking from a neurological point of view. McGilchrist writes: '… both anxiety and narrowly focussed attention engage the left hemisphere and each drives the other'.[6]

Jesus says that our heavenly Father knows our needs. In light of that, many of us have on countless occasions prayed, as the Lord taught His disciples to in the preceding verses: 'Our Father in heaven … give us this day our daily bread.' The emphasis on *this day* shows us that the Lord invites us to turn to Him daily in prayer for our food, and so we should. Giving

---

[6] *The Matter with Things*, p.368.

thanks to God for a meal is not just a trivial, unimportant ritual. It is an acknowledgement that we are ultimately dependent on God for our food. Yes, most of us may get our food by working, but the ability to work, and the job we have, are themselves the gift of God in the first place, and we need constantly to remind ourselves of that.

King David once wrote words similar to these words of Jesus: 'I have been young, and now am old, yet I have not seen the righteous forsaken or his children begging for bread' (Ps 37:25). There is an obvious problem here. How far can we take such statements? I am acutely aware that there are contexts in which these verses are difficult to understand and apply. After all, if our heavenly Father knows that His children need food and clothing, why then does He not always provide them? For instance, in many parts of the world there are families without enough food and water, and despairing even of life itself – maybe even having already lost children to starvation. To tell such people not to be anxious, especially if we ourselves are well-fed, would be insensitive and cruel. Are we therefore to think that these words about God supplying our needs are naïve and unrealistic?

Jesus' words were addressed to a crowd in that country at that time who, although not many wealthy, most had access to food. And, on at least two occasions, He used his supernatural power to feed large crowds. Yet, He did not always do that, even though He says that our heavenly Father knows our need. What He would say if He were addressing a crowd of starving people, we do not know. There is a deep mystery here that I do not profess to understand. The passage leaves us with many unanswered questions. That does not, however, mean that we cannot derive important principles from it that can guide the way we live in 'normal' times.

The apostle Paul experienced hunger and deprivation, and yet he was convinced that God would not only supply his need, but that of others. To the members of a relatively poor church in Philippi he wrote: 'Not that I am speaking of being in need, for I have learned in whatever situation I am to be content. I know how to be brought low, and I know how to abound. In any and every circumstance, I have learned the secret of facing plenty and hunger, abundance and need. I can do all things through him who strengthens me' (Phil. 4:11-13).

Because he had learned how to face not only the problem of want but of plenty, he could go on to say to others: 'And my God will supply every need of yours according to his riches in glory in Christ Jesus' (Phil. 4:19). Have I learned this secret of contentment?

Jesus has more to say about anxiety later in the Gospel of Matthew, where He repeats His call to His disciples not to be anxious, not now in the context of their need for food, but in the context of the fact that they will experience hatred, persecution, and even death, possibly even at the hands of parents, relatives and friends. He said to them: 'And do not fear those who kill the body but cannot kill the soul. Rather fear him who can destroy both soul and body in hell. Are not two sparrows sold for a penny? And not one of them will fall to the ground apart from your Father. But even the hairs of your head are all numbered' (Matt. 10:28-30). 'But not a hair of your head will perish' (Luke 21:18). The Lord Jesus has a different perspective on perishing from the usual one.

He is addressing the very real fear of physical death, and tells His disciples not to fear those who kill the body, but rather to replace that fear with another kind of fear: reverence for God, that leads to obeying Him whatever the cost. Jesus calls His disciples to be courageous in their witness for Him, even if they have to die for it.

As I write these words, I sense the danger of hypocrisy: what do I know about this? Very little, if anything. Yes, I have faced public disdain and mockery for my faith in Jesus, but I have never faced real physical persecution. However, I find one piece of encouragement in the earlier part of this passage in Matthew:

> 'Beware of men, for they will deliver you over to courts and flog you in their synagogues, and you will be dragged before governors and kings for my sake, to bear witness before them and the Gentiles. When they deliver you over, do not be anxious how you are to speak or what you are to say, for what you are to say will be given to you in that hour. For it is not you who speak, but the Spirit of your Father speaking through you'. (Matt. 10: 17-20)

I shall never forget meeting a Russian believer who, having told me about his horrific experiences in the Russian gulag, unexpectedly directly asked me: 'You couldn't face that, could you?' I was deeply embarrassed and didn't know how to respond. His face lit up as, seeing my perplexity, he went on: 'Neither could I. But I discovered that the Lord did not prepare me in advance to face that kind of thing, but when it happened, he came alongside and strengthened me and enabled me to face situations I would not have believed possible before.' That is exactly what Jesus told His disciples would happen – their need would be met in the critical hour but not necessarily before it.

This is deep water, and there are no easy answers to our theoretical 'what if' questions about the twin problems of evil and suffering. In my little book *Where is God in a Coronavirus World?*[7] I say that, in the end, we face the question as to whether there is enough evidence available to trust God with the ultimate solution to these issues, even though we do not see it now. I believe that the suffering of Christ Himself on the cross, and His subsequent triumphant resurrection from the dead, give us a way of coping until we get to glory, and are able to put the question to the Lord Himself.

One final point: we should never allow our failure to find a satisfactory solution to theoretical and possibly extreme problems that do not represent our personal situation at the moment, to stop us taking heed of these words of Jesus about anxiety in our situation. In fact, it is the taking heed of His teaching in everyday life, that will prepare us for the extreme situations, if, and when, they ever arise.

Back to the Sermon on the Mount, where Jesus now says something that may strike us initially as a bit strange: *'For the Gentiles seek after all these things' (Matt 6:32, emphasis added).* By 'Gentiles', He means essentially those who do not believe that there is a God and Father in heaven. Such people clearly have a desire for food, housing, and clothing, and go out to work to provide it, as you can test for yourself by asking people you meet in the street. Getting the basic necessities is their primary motivation for working. However, isn't that true of us all? Do

---

[7]   (London: The Good Book Company, 2020).

we not *seek after all these things*? The mention of *things* recalls McGilchrist's thesis, that there really is *something the matter with things*. Seeking after them is left-hemisphere stuff. Not only that, but, as we saw above, anxiety about them proceeds from the same left-brain source. Jesus wishes to move us away from this kind of narrowly focused thinking, by turning our eye to the much bigger picture, of which He is the creator.

Hence Jesus says next in the Sermon: 'The Gentiles seek ... but you seek...' That is, above and beyond the understandable and legitimate desire for the necessities of life, there is to be another priority for Jesus' disciples, which belongs to the right hemisphere. They are to 'seek *first* the kingdom of God and his righteousness'. The food, drink and clothing are not forgotten by the Lord. His promise is: 'They will be added unto you.' Here, Jesus is making a vital distinction between the *primary motivation*, the purpose (or goal) of work that is, the development of a relationship with God; and the *secondary* (yet important) *motivations* for, and outcomes (or by-products) of, work – the things that sustain us.

For many, if not most people, material things like food, clothing and housing are the primary motivation for work. However, for the follower of Christ, the primary motivation, according to Jesus Himself, is not – or should not be – material things at all. It is to get the right hemisphere into action, to see the bigger picture, and to *seek God's kingdom and His righteousness*.

4. What does that mean?

Some may react to the phrase rather negatively, as the concept of a kingdom and rule makes them think of legalistic rules and regulations, that often place a crushing and destructive burden on religious people.

God's kingdom certainly does involve Christ's rule. However, His rule is not despotic. It is the polar opposite of legalistic, religious slavery. Listen to Jesus explain it: 'Come to me, all who labour and are heavy laden, and I will give you rest. Take my yoke upon you, and learn from me, for I am gentle and lowly in heart, and you will find rest for your souls. For my yoke is easy, and my burden is light.' (Matt. 11:28-30)

This is a unique yoke that is geared, not to burden us, but to free us up to live a life suffused with well-being, and a sense of fulfilment in doing what God created us to do, in relationship with Him. It is a life that pleases the Lord, because it is characterised by righteousness and integrity.

An example may help. Many years ago, I was at a meeting of young Christians where a young man of around twenty was invited to talk about his Christian faith. Let's call him Jeff. He told us that, not long before, he had trained as an electrician. He was delighted, as a young Christian, when he landed his first job. He thought it was going well and so had no concern when, after a month or so, his boss called him into his office. However, to Jeff's surprise, the boss was clearly angry, and spoke sharply to him: 'What have you been doing?' Jeff was flustered: 'Sorry, I don't understand what you mean.' 'Well, you have completed the wiring of far fewer houses than your workmates.' 'I was not aware of that', Jeff said. 'I thought I had done really good work in the time available, since I was trying to be particularly careful with the under-floor wiring.' 'Yes', said the boss, 'that is just where you have got it wrong. Who sees under the floorboards, anyway?' Jeff did not hesitate. Showing great courage, he said: 'My Lord sees the wiring under the floorboards!' He was fired on the spot. Happily, he found new and satisfying employment soon afterwards.

Through his action, Jeff demonstrated that there were some things in life more important than his job security. I do not know what ultimate effect that had on the boss, but such a courageous Christian moral stand, is often the first step in someone who sees it coming to faith in Christ.

After listening to Jeff, I remember thinking whether I, a much older Christian, had got that far. Here was a young man who understood the implications of Jesus' teaching about seeking God's kingdom. Of course, he needed and wanted his pay packet at the end of the month. Yet, for him that was a secondary motivation. His primary motivation was his determination to be upright and righteous, and thus honour his relationship with the Lord in his work. Jeff had drawn a line in his mind and heart – a line he would not cross. He therefore made sure that all the hidden underfloor wiring would be done in such a way that there would be no fire risk.

Do I have a line that I will not cross? Do you? Daniel had one, as we see from Daniel 1, where he refused to compromise with idolatry by drinking the king's wine and eating his food. He would and did not cross it, and God honoured him.[8] We need a line, for, if we don't have one, we will fall. Our prime motivation should be, as Paul explains in Colossians 3:23: 'Whatever you do, work heartily, as for the Lord and not for men.'

Or, as Jesus puts it in Matthew 6, when we pray, we should say: 'Our Father in heaven, hallowed be your name. Your kingdom come ...' This captures the essence of what it means to seek God's kingdom. We are to hallow, that is make holy, or set apart, the name of the Lord. That means He is to be the supreme value, against which we measure the moral quality of our behaviour and character. He intends our work to play a major role in shaping that character, and thus honour Him.

The fundamental principle here is that of accountability. It is our accountability to the Lord that should determine our attitude and response in every situation.

At a very different level, I once heard of a senior executive, a Christian, who applied for a top position. After a very successful interview he was offered the position and accepted it. As the committee were clearing up, their most senior member took the man aside and quietly said to him: 'You will, of course, become a mason.' 'No,' was the quiet but firm reply. 'Then there is no room for you in our company'. He left without the job.

He was not prepared, for business advantage, to join a quasi-secret society that paid lip service to that strange eclectic god, Jahbulon.[9] In his refusal he was following the stance taken long ago by the Christian believers in cities like Corinth, who were tempted to join one of the many guilds in order to gain business advantage. However, membership of such guilds often involved participation in ceremonies,

---

[8] See the discussion of this in my book *Against the Flow* (Oxford: Lion-Hudson, 2015)

[9] An amalgam of Yahweh, God of Israel, Bul or Bel, a god of the Babylonians, and On, a god of the Egyptians.

where food was eaten that was sacrificed to pagan deities. Paul pointed out to the Corinthians that they could not take the financial benefit without being spiritually involved, and therefore compromised.[10]

One way to help us put this into practice is to ask ourselves in every situation we find ourselves in: what does it mean to please the Lord now?

Once we have grasped this principle, we begin to see just how important our work is. This principle applies to all work, both paid and unpaid. The factory machinist, truck driver, mechanic, builder, miner, teacher, nurse, parents looking after their children or relatives, youth pastor, Sunday school teacher, minister, missionary, etc., etc., though their activities are very different, they are all workers and are to ensure that they consciously and conscientiously do their work as unto the Lord.

Dorothy Sayers wrote: 'Work is not, primarily, a thing one does to live, but the thing one lives to do. It is, or it should be, the full expression of the worker's faculties, the thing in which he finds spiritual, mental and bodily satisfaction, and the medium in which he offers himself to God.'[11]

Os Guinness helps us apply Jesus' teaching in Matthew 6 by posing a series of questions: 'Do you allow money to dominate your priorities, assessments, relationships, and time? Do you allow consumer society to contrive your wants? Or do you do what you do, above all, for God's sake and the sheer love of it? Are you so free from anxiety about money that you can be carefree in giving to those in need? Listen to Jesus of Nazareth; answer his call.' Guinness warns, however: 'Neither work nor career can be fully satisfying without a deeper sense of call – but "calling" itself is empty and indistinguishable from work unless there is Someone who calls.'[12]

That Someone exists. There is a Lord who calls us to make the objective of work His rule and righteousness in our lives. This is a high calling that imparts to our work a

---

[10]   See 1 Corinthians 8; 1 Corinthians 10 and 2 Corinthians 6:14-18.

[11]   Dorothy L. Sayers, from "Why Work?" in *Letters to a Diminished Church: Passionate Arguments for the Relevance of Christian Doctrine* (Nashville: Thomas Nelson, 2004).

[12]   Os Guinness, *The Call*, (Nashville: Word Publishing, 1998).

real sense of dignity. Whatever our work, we are to do it as accountable to the Lord, seeking His righteousness and desiring to develop our moral integrity. We may learn things about morality in church but the main arena for building that morality into our characters, for most of us, is at work, not in the church, unless that is our sphere of operation. It is there that we face innumerable different situations with their challenges and attendant emotions: we wonder about how we are valued, we can be envious of those promoted above us, we can be dissatisfied with our salary and conditions, we can be stressed because we are overwhelmed with leadership responsibilities, or we may feel too much is being demanded of us by our bosses, we can be pressured into cutting moral corners in order to increase the bottom line, we can be treated unreasonably, we can make mistakes, we may be concerned about job security with the next takeover, we may be made redundant, be 'between jobs' or not even have a job ... The list is endless.

Each situation will test our character. It is one thing to be told from the pulpit to be patient, it is quite another to be a teacher facing a large class of children who do not seem to wish to learn, or to be an employer having to negotiate with unions, or to be responsible for looking after an elderly relative with dementia, or a disabled child, to say nothing of navigating the many temptations that work will inevitably bring. All of these things will give us the opportunity to focus our minds on the purpose of work – seeking God's kingdom and righteousness.

Basil the Great, Bishop of Caesarea (330-379AD) had a clear sense of the importance of integrating work with prayer. He wrote:

> Thus, in the midst of our work can we fulfill the duty of prayer, giving thanks to Him who has granted strength to our hands for performing our tasks and cleverness to our minds for acquiring knowledge ... praying that the work of our hands may be directed toward its goal, the good pleasure of God.

We should notice in passing that seeking God's kingdom at work does not necessarily mean, for instance, sending an email to our colleagues every morning with a Bible text for the day, or preaching over the factory intercom system! That probably would be highly counterproductive and off-putting, to say nothing of contravening rules governing use of work time and facilities. No, what we are talking about is seeking God's rule *in the work itself*, by doing it as for Him. For God is interested, in who we are, much more than in what we do. His desire is to mould our character

Nor, if we do that, will it necessarily mean that we enjoy constant success, without suffering or loss. Recall Paul's statement that we mentioned above: 'In any and every circumstance, I have learned the secret of facing plenty and hunger, abundance and need. I can do all things through him who strengthens me' (Phil. 4:12-13). That statement is very challenging indeed. Can I really say something like that with any degree of credibility?

In the seventeenth century, eight years after the Mayflower set sail for the New World, Anne Bradstreet left England to settle in the then American colonies. Life there turned out to be a very hard grind for herself, her husband Simon, and their eight children. Yet she found solace in writing poetry of such quality that she is celebrated today as the outstanding female poet of the era. Her trust in God shines through a poem that she wrote towards the end of her life, when her house and all-important library were destroyed by fire:

> And when I could no longer look,
> I blest His name that gave and took,
> That laid my goods now in the dust;
> Yea, so it was, and so 'twas just.
> It was His own; it was not mine.

That puts the gold standard of real faith in God better than I ever could. For Paul, and for Anne Bradstreet, the gifts could come and go – the Giver was the utterly dependable constant.

It is of crucial importance that God is interested in the humblest of people and their work. Think of Brother Lawrence, a 17th-century French monk who wrote a famous little book, The Practice of the Presence of God, that has been profoundly influential. Of peasant origin and poorly educated, he never became a priest. For years he cleaned and cooked in the priory kitchen. His health began to fail and he was given the job of repairing the monks' sandals. About his humble work he wrote:

> 'We ought not to be weary of doing little things for the love of God, who regards not the greatness of the work, but the love with which it is performed. And it is not necessary to have great things to do. I turn my little omelette in the pan for the love of God.'

How easy it is to focus on the greatness of the work and neglect the much more important matter of the love with which it is performed.

5. Work and Evangelism

Most work brings us into contact with others and, if our work is not exclusively with Christian believers, it gives us a ready-made sphere of evangelism that would never exist inside the walls of a church. Our colleagues and fellow workers are a network in which God has placed us as witnesses by how we live (in character), and what we say to them about the gospel when we get the opportunity. The fact that we are working alongside them gives us credentials, and an entrée that others do not have, which God expects us to use for His purposes. For instance, the fact that I am a mathematician has opened many doors of witness for me, that would be shut to other people. I find that many people are intrigued to find a scientist who believes in God, and they wish to know why. When asked in this way, I am happy to respond – for this is very different from me taking the initiative, and trying to impose my views on them.

My position as a professor of mathematics at Oxford has led to invitations to speak, debate, and proclaim the Christian message, in all sorts of forums around the world. The fact that science has considerable cachet means that I get opportunities that I might never have had, if my qualifications had been in a non-scientific field. Of course, the converse is true – there are opportunities I will not get, precisely because I am a scientist. All of us need to think constructively about how we can use our positions as a platform for evangelism, in the way that might not necessarily be open to others. God certainly intends that we should do so.

That is, if we have those kinds of credentials. Many, if not most believers do not. Indeed, many, if not most, of the early disciples did not, and far from hindering their witness, on occasions it frequently facilitated it. Recall the case of the reaction of the religious authorities in Jerusalem to the healing of the crippled man at the gate of the temple: 'Now when they saw the boldness of Peter and John, and perceived that they were uneducated, common men, they were astonished. And they recognized that they had been with Jesus' (Acts 4:13). God's power is not limited by lack of human credentials. In fact, one of the most powerful evangelists I ever met, not only had no credentials, but, converted as an adult, he had to go to school with young children to learn to read and write. God is not dependent on our credentials!

Indeed, at this point you may well ask: isn't there a risk here of trusting your credentials, or your wealth, and not the Holy Spirit, to work in peoples' hearts? Yes, there is. Trusting anything other than God is idolatry, and the way to avoid it is to distinguish between trusting your credentials or wealth, and using God (when you get stuck, as you will, at times) and trusting God, and using your credentials or wealth.

Paul was a brilliant man. In order to get a hearing for his message, he did not hesitate to use his credentials as a professional rabbi, educated in the famous elite school of Gamaliel (Acts 22:3). But the secret of his spiritual authority was that, although he *used* his credentials, he never *trusted* them: his trust was in God. We need constantly to remind ourselves of this. The way we use our credentials is important. Some people are pushy with their credentials, which can reek of pride, and be quite nauseating, and very off-putting. Others may be shy of using their credentials at all, and thereby miss opportunities for witness that they could otherwise have had. It is worthwhile sitting down and thinking carefully about our own qualifications and credentials – if we have them – and working out how we might use them in our witness. Let us, however, have our confidence firmly rooted in the Lord.

Doing our work as unto the Lord will therefore mean, not only doing it with integrity to the best of our ability but will mean having a responsibility to prayerfully look for opportunities to witness to our fellow employees/workers/colleagues, as and when we can credibly do so. There will sometimes be other Christians at our workplace with whom we can join forces, and think of innovative joint ways of getting the Christian message across to work colleagues.

This has resulted in the fact that many companies, schools, colleges, universities, hospitals, etc, in the UK have got active Christian groups, whose witness has been very effective over the years.[13]

6. An Example from the Old Testament

A vivid illustration of the difference between the ultimate motivation for, and the outcomes or by-products of work, is to be found in the experience of Israel at the time they were delivered from Egypt, and started their long journey to Canaan under the leadership of Moses. They had been oppressed by the Egyptians and forced to work unpaid, one would imagine, in slave labour camps for many years, building store and treasure cities for the Egyptians. Eventually, God through Moses, challenged the then Pharoah to let the people go, so that they could worship Him in freedom. After a series of powerful supernatural signs, finishing with Passover night, they set out under Moses' leadership to cross the sea and travel to the promised land.

As they left, they were commanded by God through Moses to 'spoil the Egyptians'. After all, they had been working as slaves for many years, and God insisted that they were compensated for it, by being given gold and valuables by their Egyptian oppressors. They took this 'back pay' with them. There being no banks, or safe-deposit boxes in those days, it was common to shape the gold or silver one possessed, into earrings that were not easy to steal.

On the desert journey, Moses was summoned to appear alone before God in the mountainous region of Sinai and,

---

[13] Evangelism brings its own special challenges, particularly that of fear, which is why I have written my small book, *Have No Fear* (10 of Those, 2020).

after he had been gone from the Israelite camp for a while, and did not seem to be returning, the people grew restive, and asked Aaron the High Priest to 'make them some gods'. Aaron gave in to their pressure, and asked them for some of their gold and silver, and fashioned a golden calf from it, in the crude, ancient pagan manner. He then announced to them: 'These are the gods that brought you up out of Egypt.' And the foolish, headstrong people, fell into idolatry and worshipped the golden calf. What use is a god that you have to carry, when there is a true God who can, and will, carry you?

For the Israelites, the gold and silver were one outcome of their redemption out of Egypt. Aaron now makes 'gods' out of them so that they become the purpose of redemption, instead of the God who called them out to Himself, as His purpose. Worse still, he even says that these gods were the means of their redemption.

That was tragic and we can see the same, (literally) half-brained mistake of turning things into gods, perpetuated today. For instance, everywhere Christianity has gone, it has brought with it education, health and often economic prosperity. With the passage of time, however, these things – education, health and prosperity – often become the central purpose of life, and are even understood to be the means of 'salvation', and God gets completely forgotten. That is very sad, since it means that the real aim and purpose of work is missed. Once again, with Iain McGilchrist, we see that there is something the matter with things! Worse still, things may tyrannise us. Emancipation from them is not easy.

There is another problem lurking here. It is the fact that Christianity has brought benefits to people, and reversed their fortunes in simple and important ways: money formerly wasted on alcohol and drugs now puts food on the table, in the home of the addict who has become a Christian. That kind of outworking of the gospel message is real evidence that Christianity is true.

However, it is very different from the so-called 'prosperity gospel', where persuasive speakers promise people, often poor people, greatly enhanced incomes, if only they will become Christians: not to mention the request to make a substantial donation to keep the preacher's own flamboyant lifestyle afloat. Neither Jesus, Paul, nor any of the early apostles did anything of that kind – the only person who got near it was the apostate Judas.

Judas was not the only one. Paul warned Timothy about people like Judas who imagine:

> that godliness is a means of gain. But godliness with contentment is great gain, for we brought nothing into the world, and we cannot take anything out of the world. But if we have food and clothing, with these we will be content. But those who desire to be rich fall into temptation, into a snare, into many senseless and harmful desires that plunge people into ruin and destruction. For the love of money is a root of all kinds of evils. It is through this craving that some have wandered away from the faith and pierced themselves with many pangs. But as for you, O man of God, flee these things. Pursue righteousness, godliness, faith, love, steadfastness, gentleness. Fight the good fight of the faith. (1 Tim. 6:5-12)

In light of all of this it is important for all of us to conduct an audit of our lives from time to time, and ask ourselves: what is my motivation and aim for my work at the moment?

As we do so, perhaps one of the most important principles is the very ancient one that, if we have wealth, it is God who has given us the power to get it:

> Beware lest you say in your heart, "My power and the might of my hand have gained me this wealth." You shall remember the Lord your God, for it is he who gives you power to get wealth, that he may confirm his covenant that he swore to your fathers, as it is this day. And if you forget the Lord your God and go after other gods and serve them and worship them, I solemnly warn you today that you shall surely perish. Like the nations that the Lord makes to perish before you, so shall you perish, because you would not obey the voice of the Lord your God. (Deut. 8:17-20)

Questions

1. What in your opinion is the most popular motivation for work? What is your motivation? Please be honest with yourself and not simply pious!

2. What indications are there that Scripture is sensitive to the feelings of the unemployed?
3. If you have been, or are unemployed, discuss what you found helpful, and what you did not find helpful in coping with the situation?
4. What makes you anxious regarding your work and your future?
5. 'You cannot serve God and money' – but you can serve God and use money, or you can serve money and use God. Discuss.
6. Discuss the meaning of 'Seek first the kingdom of God and His righteousness', giving examples of how you have experienced this in your work.
7. Do you have a line that you will not cross? What is it?
8. How do you think work can shape character? Discuss examples from experience.
9. Share experiences of opportunities to share the gospel as a result of work situations or contacts?

CHAPTER 3

A FISHERMAN SEEKS GOD'S KINGDOM

PETER THE FISHERMAN

Seeking first God's kingdom in their work was something that the early disciples had to learn. They were involved in various kinds of work: some were fishermen, one was a tax-collector, another was a political activist, and Jesus Himself was a carpenter. They were all grown men when Jesus called them to follow Him, and the circumstances of their call give us further insight into the biblical understanding of work. Luke records what happened with Simon Peter the fisherman, and some of his colleagues:

> On one occasion, while the crowd was pressing in on him to hear the word of God, he was standing by the lake of Gennesaret, and he saw two boats by the lake, but the fishermen had gone out of them and were washing their nets. Getting into one of the boats, which was Simon's, he asked him to put out a little from the land. And he sat down and taught the people from the boat. And when he had finished speaking, he said

to Simon, 'Put out into the deep and let down your nets for a catch.' And Simon answered, 'Master, we toiled all night and took nothing! But at your word I will let down the nets.' And when they had done this, they enclosed a large number of fish, and their nets were breaking. They signalled to their partners in the other boat to come and help them. And they came and filled both the boats, so that they began to sink. But when Simon Peter saw it, he fell down at Jesus' knees, saying, 'Depart from me, for I am a sinful man, O Lord.' For he and all who were with him were astonished at the catch of fish that they had taken, and so also were James and John, sons of Zebedee, who were partners with Simon. And Jesus said to Simon, 'Do not be afraid; from now on you will be catching men.' And when they had brought their boats to land, they left everything and followed him. (Luke 5:1-11)

This is a story about fishermen at work on the Sea of Galilee. Two boats had been engaged in night fishing and were now pulled up by the shore. The fishermen were washing their nets in the lake when Jesus asked Simon, who owned one of the boats, to pull it out a bit from the shore, so that He could use it as a pulpit from which to teach the people. Luke tells us nothing of what Jesus preached. His story has to do with what happened when Jesus had finished speaking. Jesus told Simon to take the boat out from the shore into deeper water and let down the nets for a catch.

Simon must have been surprised at such a strange instruction. After all, he was an expert fisherman, and fishing should be done at night and, what was worse, he and his colleagues had been working all night and caught nothing. And what would Jesus, a carpenter, know about it anyway? Simon didn't quite say it; after all, by this time, he was a converted man – but he implied it. It was pointless to try now to fish in the daylight. Yet something made Simon hesitate and, in spite of his inner reservations, he said to Jesus: 'But *at your word* I will let down the nets.'

Simon Peter meant what he said: the only reason he let down the nets was because Jesus had commanded it. Peter was not letting them down to catch fish, since he didn't believe there were any there to be caught. He was simply obeying Jesus' command. That is, for the first time in his life, so far as we know, he was going to work, not to catch fish, but because Christ the King told him to go. He was seeking Christ's kingdom rule in his life.

The effect overwhelmed him. Suddenly, the nets were bursting with fish to such an extent that they had to call the second boat to help, and even then, the sheer weight of their catch threatened to sink both vessels. Peter's reaction is noteworthy. He fell to his knees in front of Jesus and said: 'Depart from me, for I am a *sinful man*, O Lord.'

Peter was convicted of sin, not, be it noted, in a church service, or even during the sermon he had just heard, but at his work. He sensed his inadequacy, his failure to have recognized who Jesus was, and what powers He commanded. He was overwhelmed by the revelation of a big picture of whose existence he had been completely unaware. He felt that he fell very far short – that is, he was a sinner.

It could be that at work is where we, too, might well be convicted of sin.

This dramatic experience marked a turning point for Peter and his workmates, James and John: 'For he and all who were with him were astonished at the catch of fish that they had taken, and so also were James and John, sons of Zebedee, who were partners with Simon. And Jesus said to Simon, "Do not be afraid; from now on you will be catching men" And when they had brought their boats to land, they left everything and followed him.' (Luke 5:9-11).

Having learned to obey Jesus in their daily work as fishermen, they were ready to move on to something new at Jesus' direction. He now called them to leave that profession and work closely with Him.

This story contains a transformative principle that, when understood and put into practice, can add new depth, meaning and purpose to our work: 'But at your word...' Let me ask a direct and personal question of my readers and myself: when was the last time you and I went to work with an active sense that the Lord was sending us there?

We may do that by pausing at the beginning of each day and praying: 'Lord, I am off to work now. I believe that you have given me this work for a purpose. Please help me today to learn something of your rule in my life as I seek to do my job righteously and conscientiously.' Rico Tice captures this in the advice he gives to people to say to themselves: 'Today is a great day, because today is a day God has planned for me and, if it is good for God, it is good for me.' He then cites Paul: 'And we know that for those who love God all things work together for good, for those who are called according to his purpose' 88

(Rom. 8:28). This is what Rico calls 'living out the middle tense of salvation': the three tenses being, 1. Past: I have been saved (justification); 2. Present: I am being saved (sanctification); 3. Future: I shall be saved (glorification). Our day is in God's hands, so let's live it for His glory.

Preparing in this way leads to an expectation that God will work, and it increases our spiritual sensitivity to what may arise in the course of the day.

For instance, as a teacher I had to mark a great deal of mathematics homework. I was sometimes appalled at the lack of effort (rather than ability) that some students appeared to put into it. Once, I thought, this is the worst ever, yet before I went into class to confront the student in question, I prayed my prayer: 'But at your word ...' I set the work before the student and, rather than saying, something sharp and critical, I said: 'You know, I have never in the past had homework as bad as this from you and, before I say anything about it, I would just like to ask if anything has happened that would explain why it is like that.' The student teared up and said: 'Dad came home last night, hit my mum quite brutally and shouted that he was leaving her. He stomped out and was gone. I now have to cope with my devastated mum. I'm sorry ...'

I was grateful to the Lord for preventing me from making matters far worse, by heaping undeserved criticism on that student. Not only that, but my milder reaction enabled me later to have a conversation with her, at her request, about the resource that Christ had to offer in such circumstances.

I needed, and still often need, to be taught patience. Work is designed to do that for you. It will, if only you are prepared to let it.

MORALITY IN THE WORKPLACE

It will not have escaped us that seeking God's kingdom is inseparably connected with seeking His righteousness. For there is not a job in the world, paid or unpaid, that does not sooner or later – and usually sooner – raise moral questions. In my story about Jeff, it only took a few days for the moral corruption of the boss to surface. Moral issues can be of many kinds, but they usually stem from three main sources: money, sex and power. Furthermore, there is the recurrent matter of injustice in the workplace which we shall look at separately.

Money and the Workplace

Money is not evil, according to the Bible, but it is a root of a great deal of evil. This was the issue in the case of the electrician Jeff. His boss was greedy and, in his desire to make a quick killing, he not only cut moral corners himself but tried to force his workers to do so as well. Jeff resisted. If he had been prepared to go along with the boss, no doubt he could have made more money. But at what cost? The high cost of his moral integrity. In the light of God's kingdom, it wasn't worth it.

Think of it this way. Jeff's goal was honouring the Lord by seeking God's rule in his life. The boss' main aim was money. For Jeff, the money was the outcome of his work, so that compared with honouring the Lord it was a side issue, though an important one. The temptation was, and always is for any of us, to make the monetary reward for work our all-consuming aim, and, by cutting moral corners, thereby to lose the whole reason God entrusted us with the work in the first place.

The principle is the same no matter what quantity of money is involved. A Christian Chief Financial Officer may be pressurised by a company director to increase shareholder value by doing some 'creative accounting' that effectively robs the tax authorities of their lawful dues. To resist may cost him his job, and create great anxiety about his future capacity to provide for his family. As he faces his decision, he needs to know that God is interested, above all, in his maintenance of his integrity.

Power and the Workplace

According to Genesis, the first humans were gardeners, and it was in their garden workplace that they first faced the temptation to abandon God's rule, and righteousness. The temptation had to do with the produce of the garden. God told them that they could freely eat the fruit of all the trees, except for one, the tree of the knowledge of good and evil. If they were to eat the fruit of that tree, God said, they would surely die. The counter-attack by God's arch-enemy was first to call into question what God had said: 'Has God said that you shall surely die?' Then to deny it: 'You shall not surely die. God knows that in the day you eat of it you will be as gods, knowing good and evil.' The fruit looked desirable as a food, it was pleasing to their God-given aesthetic sense, and it promised wisdom. God's enemy offered them a power trip, and those three levels of attraction were enough to swamp out God's warning voice. They took the fruit, ate it, and died – not at first in the physical sense, that would come later, but the highest thing in life. Their relationship with the Creator himself, was ruptured, and their searing guilt caused them to flee from the one who up until now had been their friend. It was spiritual death.

This story is frequently misunderstood as demonstrating that God is against knowledge, since knowledge is power; that God wished, like most dictators, to suppress people, crush their initiative, and keep them from developing their full potential. That view is a slander on the name of God. For the forbidden fruit did not grow on a tree of *knowledge*. It grew on the tree of the *knowledge of good and evil*, which is something entirely different. It represents, not knowledge in general, but a specific kind of knowledge you do not want to have. God is not against knowledge, as the surrounding text shows. The garden and its surroundings were replete with potential for gaining knowledge. God encouraged them to do precisely that. They could work and explore to their hearts' content. They could explore the rivers, and discover where they led, they could develop the mineral wealth, and they could name the animals.

The tree of the knowledge of good and evil was there for a very special and important reason: not to oppress humans, but to dignify them by enabling them to develop as moral beings. Two things are essential for that to happen:
1.   A certain degree of freedom – they *could* eat of all the trees;
2.   A moral limitation to that freedom – something that they had the power to do, but which was prohibited.
Beings with no freedom are no longer human: like robots, they are automata whose behaviour is determined by their programs and have, therefore no moral significance. The words 'moral character' are meaningless for them. Indeed, everything is meaningless to an automaton.

If we think about it for a moment, we can see that morality for the first humans was defined by God's word. It was God who had given them their appetite for food, their aesthetic sense, and their desire to grow in wisdom, all of them good, even wonderful things. The subtlety of the temptation was to suggest to the humans that they were missing out by obeying what God said.

The temptation occurred in an environment that was overflowing with God's provision for every human need. Theirs was no failure that could be excused by the pressures of suffering or deprivation. Furthermore, this first temptation happened in the workplace. It usually does. It is the workplace, whether at home, factory, farm, mines, shops, building sites or offices, where we usually face the challenges that shape our lives. For instance, power play happens all the time, and men and women are often tempted to set aside the usual norms of human behaviour (based on the law of God) in order to push (or, should we say, forge?) their way ahead into more senior positions. This is often effected by subtle denigration of colleagues, by slipping in the odd white lie, and, in general, by making the by-products of work their goal.

Christians are to be different. By seeking God's rule in their work, they are to act as salt and light in society, preserving it from corruption, and pointing the way to the source of the fulfilled life in Christ. This is a very effective way of witnessing to the truth of the gospel. Yet it by no means implies that believers cannot exercise power and authority in their work.

Far from it. Indeed, the Bible itself gives notable examples of such people; for example, Abraham, Joseph, David, Nehemiah and Daniel. To exercise power in the interests of others as a Christian leader, and be a role model in terms of integrity for others, is an immense privilege.

I recall once meeting a doctor who had worked as a Christian missionary overseas for many years. I asked him how he had become a Christian. He told me that early in his career he had been working in a hospital team, and noticed that one of the nurses was always cheerful, always helpful and calm, no matter what the pressure. He was intrigued and one day, after their shift, he asked her what it was about her that made her so different. She simply said two words: 'Jesus Christ'. He did not come from a Christian background, yet these two words haunted him. In the end, he dashed into a bookshop in a rainstorm, hoping that no one would recognise him, and bought a Bible. Through reading it he became a Christian.

That nurse had been salt and light at her workplace, and as a result, whether she ever found out about it or not, her attitude, and her two words, launched a lifelong missionary career.

Sex and the Workplace

Sex is a wonderful and precious gift of God. He created it and, precisely because it is so precious, He has given us in the Scriptures His Maker's instructions as to how His gift should be used, to give the maximum of enjoyment and satisfaction. When we buy a car, we all know that it would be foolish to ignore the maker's instruction handbook and put the vehicle into reverse gear at 70 miles an hour. We would probably ruin the gear-box at the very least.

The handbook that came with the car was not written to reduce our enjoyment of the car, was it? It was designed to increase that enjoyment. And the handbook that God has given to us for life and relationships, the Bible, is not given to reduce our enjoyment, but to increase it. Sex is a very powerful drive. Its powerful motors, handled incorrectly could tear us apart. The Bible does not tell us that marriage is the proper context for sex because God wants to spoil our fun. On the contrary, He wants to prevent us from spoiling ourselves and others.

Many a man or woman has ruined their marriage, torn their family lives apart and those of others, because they found a younger, more virile, and attractive person in their workplace and, without thinking about the consequences, embarked on what we euphemistically call 'an affair'. Younger workers encounter predatory senior staff who promise rewards or promotion, if only they will sleep with them. Then there is the unspeakable horror of the abuse of children by church, or charity workers, in positions of trust – and so, on and on.

The former Chief Rabbi of the UK, Emmanuel Jakobovitz, reckons that the cost to our societies of marital infidelity is incalculable, above all, in terms of the millions of children being raised in a moral wasteland, without the shelter of a loving home. 'Is it any wonder,' he writes, 'that from their number countless embittered, selfish, lonely and sometimes violent citizens, are recruited to swell the ranks of the anti-social?' Yet such is the strength of human sexual drive that counting the cost is the very last thing that would occur to some people.

In a memorably direct piece of practical advice that applies to all areas of life, Christian blogger and political analyst John Wesley Reid writes: 'Stop flirting with what you can get away with, and instead pursue the holiness that we have through Jesus Christ.'

Paul puts it this way: 'So flee youthful passions and pursue righteousness, faith, love, and peace, along with those who call on the Lord from a pure heart' (2 Tim. 2:22). As a young teenager I was once wandering idly across a field when I suddenly spotted a gigantic bull. That taught me what fleeing meant! I fled because bulls are dangerous. Bulls are not seductive; immorality is, and is even more dangerous. Fleeing is the only wise option.

Integrity in this area, both at the workplace, and in the family, is a powerful witness to the world where so many people grow up in dysfunctional families where there is no real love, affection or stability. Christian couples have the privilege of demonstrating what Christ can do for the family, and thereby attract people to the gospel.

The Example of Joseph[1]

The book of Genesis tells us about a young man who resisted sexual temptation at the workplace, Joseph. His story is justifiably famous. He was the favourite of his father Jacob, and the envy of his brothers, who nearly murdered him, but sold him as a slave to Egypt, where he was bought by one of Pharoah's senior officials, Potiphar. Joseph rapidly proved himself a highly efficient administrator, and was soon promoted to chief steward in Potiphar's palace.

Joseph had the status of a slave in a culture that did not assign much value to human life but we, nevertheless, should not think of his situation in terms of the awful form of slavery that was abolished by the tireless work of the Christian social activist William Wilberforce and the Clapham Group in the Slavery Abolition Act of 1833. Earlier still in Old Testament times, it is recorded that it sometimes happened that slaves actually had some affection for their masters to the extent that they said: 'I don't want to go free. I want to serve you.' That was very rare and differnt from the awful dehumanising, brutal slavery against which Wilberforce campaigned.

However, in spite of such efforts, it is a deeply distressing scandal that there are still many slaves in the world today, men, women and children, suffering indescribably in the most inhuman conditions. Their numbers are thought to run into millions. They are even to be found in the most 'civilised' of Western nations including, I regret to say, the United Kingdom, where slave victims of human trafficking are regularly discovered.

Joseph clearly enjoyed considerable freedom when he became head steward of Potiphar's house. Potiphar seems to have been prepared to trust people, when he saw evidence that they could be trusted. In contemporary terms, Joseph became a high-powered administrator and manager of a large organisation.

---

[1] For more on this, see my book, *Joseph: A Story of Love, Hate, Slavery, Power and Forgiveness*, (Wheaton: Crossway, 2019).

Potiphar rapidly discovered that his confidence in Joseph was well-placed. His house was blessed by the Lord, so that Potiphar did not have to bother about anything other than the food he ate, a side comment that confirms the authenticity of the Genesis document. Egyptians at the time are known to have been fussy about their food.

It will not have escaped our attention that Joseph's public witness took place in the workplace, and his story is therefore relevant to the broader question of our own attitude as Christian believers to work, and the workplace.

We saw in our brief introduction to Genesis that work was intended by the Creator to be an integral part of human life. God assigned to the first humans the work of tending a garden. It was an idyllic workplace where they enjoyed the immediate fellowship of God, as they went about their activities. All that lay in the distant past, when Joseph entered his 'employment' as steward in Potiphar's palace. Sin had long since entered the world, and brought with it damage to all levels of life. Work was now characterised by an element of toil. The environment was no longer idyllic. Thorns and thistles, both literal and metaphorical, had sprung up. Think, for instance, of the unfairness of Joseph's situation. Nevertheless, he maintained a dignity, poise and integrity that transcended the bitterness that would characterise many of us in his situation.

Yet, we are to understand that 'the Lord was with him', and I am sure that Joseph himself was aware of it. As a result, his whole demeanour showed that he did his work not simply for Potiphar, but ultimately for his God. This is a vitally important principle whose equivalent is emphasised in the New Testament, for Christians. Paul writes: 'Whatever you do, work heartily, as for the Lord and not for men, knowing that from the Lord you will receive the inheritance as your reward. You are serving the Lord Christ' (Col. 3:23-24). The operative word here is 'whatever'. The Lord is interested in every aspect of our lives, and not simply in what we think of as our spiritual activities. Our daily work is to be done for Him. He is interested in what we do at the workbench. After all, God's Son was a carpenter. In order to grasp what this means, just imagine what it would feel like if Jesus were to appear to us personally, and say: 'I wonder, could you do this for me?' Would we not be overwhelmed with a sense of privilege and responsibility? Well, He speaks directly to us through His word, so surely our reaction should be with the same sense of privilege and responsibility?

Not only was God with Joseph, Potiphar sensed it, whatever he made of it. Joseph's attitude to his work, and his boss, were a witness to the reality of his faith in God. This led to deepening trust, and Potiphar became so pleased with Joseph that he gave him a free hand in running the estate. However, with that trust and freedom came danger. Potiphar's wife, who we assume must have been a very attractive Egyptian woman, noticed the handsome young man Joseph – taking after his mother Rachel, no doubt – and, because they were often alone together in the house, she started flirting with him, and eventually tried to seduce him into sleeping with her. It was a major temptation not only for sex, but also, in that ancient society, could well have paved the way for Joseph to attain power. Many a contemporary psychologist would have urged Joseph, young and full of hormones as he was, to go for it and enjoy himself. Why not?

Yet Joseph refused and gave his reasons for so doing. He said to Potiphar's wife: 'Behold, because of me my master has no concern about anything in the house and he has put everything that he has in my charge. He is not greater in this house than I am, nor has he kept back anything from me except you, because you are his wife. How then can I do this great wickedness and sin against God?' (Gen. 39:8-9).

However, she would not desist and, eventually, grabbed him and tried to pull him down beside her, but he tore away, left his garment in her hand, and fled. One can see at once how similar, and yet how different, the situation here is to that of the temptation described in Genesis 3. Then it was a beautiful garden, here a beautiful palace, then there was one thing forbidden, the fruit of the tree of knowledge of good and evil, that the woman offered the man, here it was the woman offering herself as the forbidden fruit. Yet Adam gave in to the temptation; he was not prepared to reject the fruit because in so doing he would be rejecting the woman. Joseph did not give in. He was prepared to reject the woman. Why? Because she did not belong to him. She was someone else's wife, and Joseph knew that to take her would be to violate God's word. He knew the difference between good and evil, and he refused the evil.

The fact that they were alone, and no one could see them made no difference to Joseph's decision. His ethics were not situational. He knew that God could see him, as God could see under Jeff's floorboards. Seeking the kingdom of God meant that Joseph did the right thing in the eyes of God. He regarded himself as accountable to the Lord.

Joseph did not fail at the workplace on this occasion. Yet, Adam and millions of others have done so. The Bible is very realistic and gives us examples of people who tragically messed up their lives in this area. Probably King David is the most famous of them. Not only did he commit adultery with Bathsheba, he abused his status as king (his work) to have her husband murdered to get him out of the way. And yet David, when faced with his sin by the prophet Nathan, repented of what he had done, and received God's forgiveness, as described in Psalm 51.

And we, in our turn, though we may well not have fallen in the same way, or as far as David did, still sin, and need to repent, and confess it to the Lord: 'If we say we have no sin, we deceive ourselves, and the truth is not in us. If we confess our sins, he is faithful and just to forgive us our sins and to cleanse us from all unrighteousness' (1 John 1:8-9). And if we sin, whether at the workplace or anywhere else, the sooner we sort it out the better. Unconfessed sin has a way of sitting on our conscience, and reducing our effectiveness in our lives in general, and in the workplace in particular. It takes courage, but can bring great relief, to go to a colleague, confess that we have wronged them, and to ask for forgiveness.

However, though forgiven the guilt of sin, neither David nor us can remove the consequences of sin. David could not bring Bathsheba's husband back to life. Sin always has consequences. Imagine, for example, that a drunk driver knocks you down, smashes your spine and leaves you a paraplegic for the rest of your life. It may be that, after some time, with God's grace and the driver's repentance, you might be prepared to forgive him, but you'll still be a paraplegic. He cannot undo the damage he caused.

Injustice and the workplace

There is more to be gleaned from the story of Joseph. After he made his remarkable moral stand, his boss, Potiphar, returned home, listened to and accepted the false accusations of his wife, that Joseph had attempted to rape her. There is no evidence that Potiphar ever heard Joseph's side of the story. He simply put him in prison. Joseph suffered for doing the right and moral thing at his workplace. There is no guarantee that we shall not experience the same sort of injustice at work.

As every parent knows, one of the first things that children seem to develop is a strong conviction about fairness – a conviction that does not necessarily go away as we get older. Indeed, most of us feel at some stage in our lives that we are being treated unfairly, very often in the workplace. One thing that life teaches us, that life isn't fair, and that there is a great deal of unfairness in the world. The question is: how do we react when the unfairness reaches us? For instance, how many of us have worked hard, only to see a colleague who has not made a great deal of effort, except in ingratiating himself with his superiors, gain a promotion, when we felt we deserved it more? How should we behave as Christians towards unreasonable superiors, who make unreasonable decisions? Should we defend ourselves? Should we stand up for our rights? Or should we just let it go?

In New Testament times a large part of the working population in the Roman Empire were slaves. They were not employees with wages and rights, although we must not imagine that they were all like the slaves who were victims of the much later inhuman slave-trade, based in Britain and elsewhere. Some of them were given hard, menial labour, but others were in skilled professions like teaching, bookkeeping and estate management.

It was also possible for some slaves to gain their freedom. However, the fact remains that they were treated as mere property by their owners. They were victims of a dehumanising social evil that would one day be largely abolished by the teaching of Christianity, in the hands of men like William Wilberforce. Yet, nowhere in the New Testament do we find slaves being encouraged to revolt against the system that had enslaved them. The biblical approach is not that of violent revolution. This does not mean that there is no criticism of slavery in the New Testament – Paul includes 'enslavers' among the 'lawless and disobedient' (1 Tim. 1:10). There was no quick fix to the evil of slavery, so thoroughly did it permeate ancient Roman society. As the Christian message spread, many slaves responded to it, and became Christians as also did some of the slave owners. There are several passages where the apostles address slaves directly. What each has to say has obvious applicability to employees as well, and is therefore very relevant for us today:

> Only let each person lead the life that the Lord has assigned to him, and to which God has called him. This is my rule in all the churches ... Were you a slave when called? Do not be concerned about it. (But if you can gain your freedom, avail yourself of the opportunity.) For he who was called in the Lord as a bondservant is a freedman of the Lord. Likewise, he who was free when called is a bondservant of Christ. You were bought with a price; do not become bondservants of men. So, brothers, in whatever condition each was called, there let him remain with God. (1 Cor. 7:17, 21-24)

In this passage, Paul applies to household slaves a principle by which he himself lived – being content with the circumstances in which he found himself, even if that was imprisonment. But they were not to do so in a purely passive way – if they could gain their freedom, then they should do so. Therefore, this passage should not be taken to mean that God will not call you into another sphere of work, as Luther thought. Miroslav Volf has written that since the factors, by which God guides people to work, may change over the course of a working life, God may indeed guide people to change their work.

The crucial thing was that they should behave as 'bond-slaves of Christ'. That was to be reflected in the believing slave's servant attitude to his or her boss, so that the reputation of Christianity was enhanced:

> Let all who are under a yoke as slaves regard their own masters as worthy of all honour, so that the name of God and the teaching may not be reviled. Those who have believing masters must not be disrespectful on the ground that they are brothers; rather they must serve all the better since those who benefit by their good service are believers and beloved. Teach and urge these things. (1 Tim. 6:1-2)

> Bondservants, obey your earthly masters with fear and trembling, with a sincere heart, as you would Christ, not by the way of eye-service, as people-pleasers, but as bondservants of Christ, doing the will of God from the heart, rendering service with a good will as to the Lord and not to man, knowing that whatever good anyone does, this he will receive back from the Lord, whether he is a slave or free. Masters, do the same to them, and stop your threatening, knowing that he who is both their Master and yours is in heaven, and that there is no partiality with him. (Eph. 6:5-9)

> Masters, treat your slaves justly and fairly, knowing that you also have a Master in heaven. (Col.4:1)

Each of these passages shows that sometimes a believing slave would be in the service of a believing master. In terms of application for today, the important thing here, says Paul, is that an employee must not use the fact that he or she is a Christian brother or sister of the employer as an excuse to be disrespectful. Sadly, this happens all too often and can create great tension, as can the opposite situation, where Christian employers deliberately and unfairly underpay their employees, or pay them late. Sad anywhere, but particularly sad if Christian believers are involved.

The apostle James is devastating in his critique of such practices wherever they are to be found:

> Come now, you rich, weep and howl for the miseries that are coming upon you. Your riches have rotted and your garments are moth-eaten. Your gold and silver have corroded, and their corrosion will be evidence against you and will eat your flesh like fire. You have laid up treasure in the last days. Behold, the wages of the labourers who mowed your fields, which you kept back by fraud, are crying out against you, and the cries of the harvesters have reached the ears of the Lord of hosts. You have

lived on the earth in luxury and in self-indulgence. You have fattened your hearts in a day of slaughter. You have condemned and murdered the righteous person. He does not resist you. (Jas. 5:1-6)

If Christian employers have that kind of attitude, their professed faith counts for nothing. Their behaviour gets noticed, not only on earth but by a master in heaven. It isn't worth it as we shall later see when we consider the matter of reward. Reputation matters.

The New Testament also contains a priceless letter to a certain Philemon, a friend of Paul who owned a slave Onesimus who ran away. We are not told why he did that – it may even be that Philemon had treated him unfairly. While he was on the run, Onesimus met Paul, who was imprisoned at the time. Paul led him to Christ and sent him back to Philemon bearing a letter asking him to receive the slave as a brother and no longer as a slave, indeed asking him to welcome Onesimus in the same way as he would have welcomed his friend Paul. Paul was even prepared to compensate Philemon for any loss he had sustained through Onesimus. Paul's letter is a gem of Christian sensitivity to the existing social structure, yet it contains within it the living seeds that eventually undermined and largely put an end to an inhuman practice.

Finally, Jesus Himself came into contact with slaves. Luke records, firstly, that He healed the slave belonging to a Roman centurion (Luke 7:1-10) and secondly, that He healed the ear of the high priest's servant that had been severed by a sword foolishly wielded by Peter (Luke 22:51). Yet, above everything else it is the example of the Lord when He suffered, that is to be borne in mind when a slave, employee, or anyone else is being treated unjustly.

Here is what the apostle Peter had to say about it:

Servants, be subject to your masters with all respect, not only to the good and gentle but also to the unjust. For this is a gracious thing, when, mindful of God, one endures sorrows while suffering unjustly. For what credit is it if, when you sin and are beaten for it, you endure? But if when you do good and suffer for it you endure, this is a gracious thing in the sight of God. For to this you have been called, because Christ also suffered for you, leaving you an example, so that you might follow in his steps. He committed no sin, neither was deceit found in his mouth. When he was reviled, he did not revile in return; when he suffered, he did not threaten, but continued entrusting himself to him who judges justly. He himself bore our sins in his body on the tree, that we might die to sin and live to righteousness. By his wounds you have been healed. For you were straying like sheep, but have now returned to the Shepherd and Overseer of your souls. (1 Pet. 2:18-25)

Peter's teaching is quite difficult for us to hear. In fact, if we are honest, there are aspects of it we don't instinctively like. Yet it is as important for us in the 21st century as it was in the 1st, even though there have been profound changes in culture. Its importance lies in the fact that most of us will experience not only just and good leadership but also management that is unjust, whether we are paid employees, or volunteers.

What then should we do in situations where we have been wronged or treated unfairly, or where we see our colleagues treated unfairly? As Christian we need to be wise in how we act. First of all, we should notice that the Lord Jesus was prepared to defend unfair treatment of others and spoke up about it – indeed, his scathing criticisms of some of the Pharisees of his day for their blatant exploitation of the poor and helpless are justifiably famous.[2] It was costly to do that because it brought down the wrath of the Pharisees on him and in our turn we must be prepared for a backlash if we speak up in the defence of others.

On the other hand, when Jesus was himself criticised, he often took it on the chin – 'the reproaches of them that reproached you fell on me' (Rom. 15:3). The Apostle Peter applies this fact to believers: Servants, be subject to your masters with all respect, not only to the good and gentle but also to the unjust. For this is a gracious thing, when, mindful of God, one endures sorrows while suffering unjustly. For what credit is it if, when you sin and are beaten for it, you endure? But if when you do good and suffer for it you endure, this is a gracious thing in the sight of God. For to this you have been called, because Christ also suffered for you, leaving you an

---

[2] See e.g. Matthew 23

example, so that you might follow in his steps. He committed no sin, neither was deceit found in his mouth. When he was reviled, he did not revile in return; when he suffered, he did not threaten, but continued entrusting himself to him who judges justly. He himself bore our sins in his body on the tree, that we might die to sin and live to righteousness. By his wounds you have been healed. For you were straying like sheep but have now returned to the Shepherd and Overseer of your souls (1 Pet. 2:18-25).

Thanks to the influence of many Christian thinkers and reformers over the centuries, workers in many, but sadly not all, situations have certain rights and may protest against unreasonable treatment. They are not, therefore, in the same position as the 'servants' or 'slaves' that Peter was addressing in that they have opportunities to speak up and defend themselves. After all, if we do not speak up or do nothing in the contemporary world where we have the ability to do so, those who treat us unfairly may think we have something to hide, especially if the unfairness involves accusations of moral failure or impropriety where it is important that we defend ourselves (that is, if we are not guilty as one might hope). There are times when we may need to confront an unjust boss, not only for our sake, but for that of others. In that situation it is vitally important that our demeanour is thoroughly Christian. We should also remember that not all anger is sinful (Eph. 4:26)!

Leadership under Pressure – Nehemiah the Building Contractor

One biblical character who also exemplifies the principles that flow from seeking God's kingdom in the workplace at the leadership level, but who is possibly not so well-known as Joseph and Daniel (about both of whom I have written elsewhere), is Nehemiah. The main message of the book that bears his name is his faithfulness to God, while working as an official government building contractor working on a very big project to rebuild the ruined city of Jerusalem, in what turned out to be very difficult circumstances.

Nehemiah introduces himself as cup-bearer to the Persian king, Artaxerxes. This meant that he was a man of impeccable integrity, since he was trusted with the king's wine in an age where poisoning wine was a favourite method of assassination, in the Ancient Near East. It is clear from his writing that the secret of that integrity was his relationship with God. Nehemiah was a man who 'feared God's name' and that reverence for God was the key to his attitude to his work.

He had heard reports that Jerusalem's walls had been broken down, and its gates burnt with fire. His heart was full of concern for Jerusalem, and he risked showing that concern on his face as he served the king. The king must have valued Nehemiah highly, since he asked the cause of the concern, and Nehemiah told him. The remarkable upshot of the conversation was a commission from the king to go and repair Jerusalem at the king's expense.

This is an outstanding example of how faithfulness in one area of work can lead to vastly greater opportunity in another area. Nehemiah set out under the protection of an army unit, provided by the king, and immediately encountered opposition from tribal leaders hostile to Israel. Undeterred, with a few trusted men, he surveyed the damage by night, after which he called the local Jewish leaders together:

> Then I said to them, 'You see the trouble we are in, how Jerusalem lies in ruins with its gates burned. Come, let us build the wall of Jerusalem, that we may no longer suffer derision.' And I told them of the hand of my God that had been upon me for good, and also of the words that the king had spoken to me. And they said, 'Let us rise up and build.' (Neh. 2:17-18)

Nehemiah was concerned about the fact that Jerusalem was being held in derision, God was being mocked and His reputation was suffering in the eyes of the world. Word got around quickly that Nehemiah intended to build, and the mockery increased. Nehemiah's attitude fits in perfectly with Peter's injunction: 'Keep your conduct among the Gentiles honourable, so that when they speak against you as evildoers, they may see your good deeds and glorify God on the day of visitation' (1 Pet. 2:12).

In this new situation Nehemiah now shows himself to be a man of formidable managerial ability, and the construction proceeded apace until it began to threaten the enemies to such an extent, that Nehemiah had not only to direct the building work, but also a major security operation to give armed protection to the builders on-site.

That was bad enough, but then he discovered that some of the local Israelite population were extorting their own people, and even enslaving them, to pay off borrowings. Nehemiah was furious. Yet, with consummate skill, he decided to denounce such practices in public, in order to shame those involved into bringing them to an end. He even managed, incredibly, to get those guilty to restore what they had taken. Finally, with his insight into human nature, he insisted on the officials swearing to do what they had promised.

Achieving this kind of thing takes a great deal of moral authority. Nehemiah had it. For the preceding 12 years (that is how long the work had taken) he had refused to take the allowance of food granted to him, as Governor of Judah, by the king.

The governors who had preceded him had laid heavy taxes on the people and oppressed them. Nehemiah did not attempt to make the kind of corrupt financial killing that is sadly so typical of those granted power. Nor did he abuse his position to acquire land – that most precious of commodities at all times. He chose an altogether simpler lifestyle than his predecessors. His reason for getting on with the work without creaming off its potential by-products was this: 'But I did not do so, because of fear of God' (Neh. 5:15).

What he did do to relieve pressure is equally remarkable:

> Moreover, there were at my table 150 men, Jews and officials, besides those who came to us from the nations that were around us. Now what was prepared at my expense for each day was one ox and six choice sheep and birds, and every ten days all kinds of wine in abundance. Yet for all this I did not demand the food allowance of the governor, because the service was too heavy on this people. Remember for my good, O my God, all that I have done for this people. (Neh. 5:17-19)

This is the same attitude that Paul adopted centuries later, in foregoing his rights and financing his own gospel work – a brilliant example of a gifted leader seeking God's righteousness at the workplace. And God will remember him for good.

As an aside, we might observe that Nehemiah was a prophet, as well as a building contractor, and a civil servant – a fact that leads us neatly into the next chapter.

Questions

1. Think of a situation in your life when you experienced what it meant to seek God's kingdom and righteousness?
2. Do you go to work with an active sense that the Lord is sending you there?
3. Discuss your experiences of moral temptation in the workplace and how you coped with it? How can we help each other face such temptations?
4. What areas do you think you need personally to work on? Do you need to seek help?
5. What is the most important lesson you have learned from the life of Joseph?
6. Share experiences of injustice in the workplace? What was it and how did you deal with it? Under what circumstances should you interfere if you see someone else being treated unjustly?
7. What lessons about leadership can we learn from Nehemiah?

CHAPTER 4

SECULAR OR SACRED?

The story with which we began the preceding chapter records a transition for Peter (and others) from one kind of work to another. Such transitions are often described as a 'call' from secular work into full-time Christian work. That notion has been, either explicitly or implicitly, set before many young Christians as the ideal to which they should aim. This, in turn, has led many people to imagine that there are, really, two classes of Christians: those who earn their keep in secular employment, and those who are employed full-time by the church, or by a Christian organisation, institution or agency.

The subtle subtext here is that the latter group are the first class Christians and the former have not quite made the grade, even though the former group is often expected to finance the latter! This view comes in part to us from the Middle Ages, when it was considered to be a 'higher' or 'holier' calling to be a priest, monk, or a nun than to be a farmer, tradesman or homemaker. We ought to realise that there was a deep problem with this, since it was (and still is) associated with the unbiblical ground rule, forbidding marriage, about which

Paul's uncompromising statement in 1 Timothy 4:3 is well known.

The upshot is that even today, and not only in Roman Catholic circles, the word 'call' is used in contexts like 'call to the ministry' or 'call to full-time Christian work'. For instance, a student wrote: 'I wanted to become a CEO, but then God called me to something greater. ... I sensed God was calling me to full-time ministry.' Very rarely do we hear 'call to work in the city'; or 'call to be' a salesman, teacher, artist, musician, nurse, IT expert; or 'call to be' at home as a parent, or carer.

This can lead to considerable tension. For instance, here is a young woman that finds she is passionate about language and literature. She studies English and gets a good degree. She is also a very keen believer who loves working with young people. When she expresses to a church leader her desire to be an English teacher at school, she is told: 'Of course, that is a worthy thing to do. But you are a gifted youth worker, and you would be so much more effective working in the church fulltime'. That piles on the pressure and creates a tension within her, between serving God and becoming a schoolteacher.

She is not told, as I would tell her, of the immense opportunities for an English teacher in a school where she can influence pupils, who may have absolutely no connection with any church, teach them to think, and bring her Christianity to bear on them, with care and sensitivity. She is not reminded, as I would remind her, of the fact that schoolteachers have generous holidays, during which, if she wishes, she can get involved in Christian youth camps, etc. Nor is she told that it is perfectly possible to help run a youth group, be a speaker and/or writer, at the same time as being a teacher in a school.

Finally, she is not told that, in any case, neither her church leader, nor I, have any right to tell her what to do. Even Peter himself, an apostle, no less, was faced with this lesson by Jesus, and it is therefore very important. At the end of the Gospel of John, in chapter 21, after the conversation in which Jesus encourages Peter to feed the sheep; the first 'sheep' that Peter sees is John. 'What shall this man do?' says Peter to Jesus. The answer, in colloquial English, is very direct: 'That is none of your business.' Peter had to learn, like pastors and the rest of us, that feeding sheep is not to be confused with controlling servants. Historically, the professing Christian church has frequently failed to understand this, and has become expert in controlling servants. However, the job of a shepherd is to feed the sheep, and bring them to Jesus, so that they respond to Him as Lord and not to anyone else. The important thing for the student in question is that she makes her career decisions before the Lord, and not because she is pressurised by me, or anyone else.

Telling others what to do is a serious business that should only be undertaken by those qualified. Paul made the necessary qualifications clear: 'To this end Christ died and lived again, that he might be Lord ...' (Rom. 14:9). That is blunt, to say the least: if we haven't both died and risen, then we had better avoid trying to control what people do!

Of course, that does not mean we do not need, or should not seek, advice and direction from pastors or anyone else – we all need to do that. It is just that those giving advice need to make sure they are doing it in such a way that they are not taking the Lord's place in another person's life. I repeat, the job of a shepherd is to lead people to the Lord, so that He tells them what to do, not to get between them and the Lord by telling them what to do himself. Yet, we find the following injunction in Hebrews: 'Obey your leaders and submit to them, for they are keeping watch over your souls, as those who will have to give an account. Let them do this with joy and not with groaning, for that would be of no advantage to you' (Heb. 13:17). And those of us who aspire to be Bible teachers need also to heed the warning of James: 'Not many of you should become teachers, my brothers, for you know that we who teach will be judged with greater strictness' (3:1).

Teachers are required to teach, and church leaders are required to lead, but it is the manner and style of their leadership that is important. Their authority is determined by the degree to which they live like Christ. Paul wrote: 'Be imitators of me, as I am of Christ' (1 Cor. 11:1). It is not always easy to get this in proportion if you are also in a secular position of authority, say, in a corporation where many others answer, look to you to be told what they have to do. For instance, here is a Christian CEO of a multinational, sitting in church. How are they to understand their relationship to the minister, or church leader? What is to be their attitude to the authority of that leader?

'Full-time' work

Over the years, I have been approached by well-intentioned people, often friends for whom I have high regard, who suggest that I should leave my university teaching and 'go into full-time work' with their organisation. Now, of course, university teaching is 'full-time' work, but this phrase has become common among Christians to represent work that solely involves Christian activity – teaching, preaching, pastoring, etc. I have usually replied: 'I am afraid you are too late.' 'Surely not,' comes the reply, 'it is never too late to go full-time.' 'You misunderstand me. I have actually been active in full-time Christian work for many years: part of it is as a university teacher of mathematics, part as a husband, part as a father, part as a Bible teacher, part engaged in the intellectual defence of the gospel, part as a friend, etc., etc. This is all work for the Lord. The problem is your definition: '"full-time Christian work" is not actually a Biblical concept as such.' Sometimes, when I enquired how much activity was really involved in this so-called full-time work, I was saddened to discover that I was doing much more, in what they would have called my spare-time.

In fact, the concept of full-time work is a dangerously misleading idea, since it might be taken to mean that there is such a thing as part-time Christian work. It then sets up an artificial secular-sacred divide (SSD) that is endemic *within* the church, and ultimately has a limiting effect on the reach of the gospel message. Mark Greene, the Director of the London Institute for Contemporary Christianity, writes:

> It is because of SSD that the vast majority of Christians feel that they do not get any significant support for their daily work, from the teaching, preaching, prayer, worship, pastoral, group aspects, of local church life. No support for how they spend fifty percent of their waking lives. As one teacher put it: 'I spend an hour a week teaching Sunday school and they haul

me up to the front of the church to pray for me. The rest of the week I'm a full-time teacher and the church has never prayed for me. That says it all.'

Read the following quotation, bearing in mind what we said above about the aspiring schoolteacher:

> It is because of SSD that a 17-year-old can go to a superb youth conference with thousands of 12 to 18-year-olds, be encouraged by stunning Bible teaching, engaged in God-honouring worship, offered life-changing prayer, given a vision for a life of service and mission, but never hear the word 'school' in relation to mission, never have the call to mission and discipleship connected to the place where they spend a huge proportion of their waking time.[1]

It is because of SSD that David Wilson, the former national leader of the evangelistic organization, Agape, could conclude, 'We teach gentle Jesus, meek and mild to teenagers in church. Meanwhile, in the world, they're studying nuclear physics. No wonder they drift away from Christianity when they go to university.'

Or: 'SSD tells us that 98 percent of us are not missionaries, ministers or full-time Christian workers. SSD tells us that all Christians may be born equal but full-time Christian workers are more equal than others. It's a lie. Did Jesus call any of us to be a part-time Christian worker? Or to take up our cross daily, but only when we get home from work or school?' Was Jesus Himself only part-time when working as a carpenter? The mind boggles.

It was the SSD that prompted a businessman to say: "The church appreciates my tithe, but not the enterprise that gave rise to it."

---

[1] https://licc.org.uk/resources/the-great-divide/

The Problem of Authority

The SSD may create confusion as regards different kinds of authority. In the church sphere, authority is vested with elders, leaders and pastors overseeing the spiritual well-being of the flock. Now think of a CEO who directs the work of thousands of employees in her business. Yet in church she may sit under the authority of leaders who know nothing of such levels of responsibility. It will take great grace on her part to learn from them and great grace on their part to take her work seriously enough to feed and guide her with what she needs. As has been well remarked: 'It is easier to feed lambs than mature sheep.'

Work as Calling

Martin Luther wrote: 'What seems to be secular works are actually the praise of God and represent an obedience which is well-pleasing to him.' Luther had a deep sense of work as calling. Indeed, the German word that is most used for describing the work a person does is *Beruf*, a word derived from the verb *rufen = to call*.

Bishop Hugh Latimer, an English Reformer who was burnt at the stake in Oxford for his faith, in 1555, reminded his fellow believers: 'Our Saviour Christ was a carpenter and got his living with great labour. Therefore, let no man disdain to follow him in a common calling and occupation. For as he blessed our nature with taking upon him the shape of man, so in his doing he blessed all occupations and arts'.

In her essay, cited earlier, Dorothy Sayers said: 'It is the business of the Church to recognize that the secular vocation, as such, is sacred. Christian people, and particularly perhaps the Christian clergy, must get it firmly into their heads that when a man or woman is called to a particular job of secular work, that is as true a vocation as though he or she were called to specifically religious work.'

Elizabeth Elliott, whose husband Jim was martyred at the age of 28 in 1956 by the Auca Indians in Ecuador, wrote: 'My house, my kitchen, my desk, my very body are meant to be holy places in this world for the eternal God'.

It is for this reason that the *Theology of Work Project* states as one of its fundamental convictions: 'We also affirm that non-church work is as much 'full-time Christian service' as church work. All Christians are called (that is, commanded) to conduct everything they do, round the clock, as full-time service to Christ: 'Whatever your task, put yourselves into it, as done for the Lord and not for your masters' (Col. 3:23).

As Os Guinness puts it: 'First and foremost we are called to Someone (God) not to something …' It is for that Someone to call us to something – whether to trade, teaching, pastoring, preaching, motherhood or voluntary work etc. – or a mixture of more than one of these.

Perhaps we should stop using the term *full-time,* and simply make the distinction between different kinds of work: e.g., farming, business, home-making and church work all of which can and should be done full-time for the Lord.

The problem of youth unemployment

There is a further major problem lurking in this general area. In some countries youth unemployment is high. It can therefore be very tempting for young people, straight out of education, with no experience of doing a job of work, where they are accountable to a manager or boss, to think that, if they are keen Christians, the thing to do is to 'go into the church' or 'go into Christian' work. They may even have been taught that 'full time' Christian work is the thing to be aimed at.

This teaching has filled them with the belief that they are entitled to the financial support of the church, or Christian organisation. This, sadly, can appear to be a soft option. The result can be disastrous. Having not had a real sense of responsibility and accountability drilled into them, by doing a straightforward job, where they are accountable for their time and expenses to a possibly non-Christian boss, they may end up content with a very poor work rate. The result is that they do far less work than others do, drifting along at others' expense, even, sadly in some instances, giving the impression that they are on permanent paid holiday – as I have personally witnessed all too often.

Here is one aspect of this danger as described from the perspective of an Asian Christian student organisation: 'There are a lot of young people, just graduated who can't seem to find that dream job. So instead of just sitting around some dead-end job, they decide that going abroad to be a missionary would be a good time killer, look good on their CV, and be a good excuse to do some travelling. They are in danger of doing mission work solely as an escape from their boring life back home. This will not give you a passion to spread the gospel, and it will certainly not continue to motivate you when you tire of the excitement of being in a new culture (this excitement usually wears off after 3-6 months but is different for each individual).'

Now I do not wish the reader to misunderstand me. Missionary outreach is of the essence of Christianity. After all, the Lord Jesus Himself founded the church, commanded the mission, backing it with His full divine authority. I also hold many Christian organisations and charities in high regard. It has been one of life's great privileges to be permitted to work with many of them.

What is very clear is that at the heart of those that thrive there are a few individuals with a deep sense of calling, who, often at considerable personal cost, maybe even to the extent of foregoing lucrative careers, devote all of their time and energy, to the service of the Lord. Nothing that I have said should lead us to think that God will not call any of us to join their ranks. The opening up of new fields for mission has always been and will always be driven by such pioneering leaders who have sometimes had to follow God's call with very little or no support from others.

I am also encouraged to find in numerous churches and organisations, many committed and active Christians who, recognising the problem I have just mentioned, teach those, for whom they are responsible, how to avoid it. They, too, would agree that it is no accident that the Lord chose as His disciples mature, work-hardened men who knew what life was all about. How often have missionaries said to me: 'I wish the churches would send out people that know how to work, and not just those with a bit of Christian education in a Bible college, and some Christian activity in the church, but with no real, character building, work experience that has produced a sense of accountability.'

What is needed, they say, is to send mature people, who have already proved themselves to be able to do their 'ordinary jobs' for the Lord.

We should note, by the way, that when Jesus called the early disciples like Peter to become 'fishers of men', that did not mean that they never engaged in their former work again. One of those men that Jesus called was Peter among his experienced fishermen friends. Jesus called him to leave his fishing, and to join Him in His mission to fish for men, so that he was subsequently financed by the Christian community. It is to be noted, however, when Peter had no clear idea of what the Lord wished him to do next, he went back to fishing to provide for himself and his family – and he was not criticised for that, as we shall see.

Questions

1. Share experiences of being made to feel a 'second-class' Christian. How can we combat this?
2. Why does the concept of 'full-time' Christian work continue to be used? For convenience, or through deep misunderstanding?
3. How can your church improve its attitude to your working week?
4. Do you view your work as 'calling'? Does that make a difference to your attitudes?
5. What, in your view, are the dangers of going directly into 'ministry' without having any normal work experience?

CHAPTER 5

GOSPEL PATRONS

We now return to the distinction we have made between the ultimate purpose of work and its by-products. The latter are many and varied. Money, of course, is one of them. There are others to which no monetary value can be assigned, most important of which is Christian character growth as described by Paul: 'But the fruit of the Spirit is love, joy, peace, patience, kindness, goodness, faithfulness, gentleness, self-control' (Gal. 5:22-23). To that we could add the accumulation of knowledge, experience and wisdom. We can think of all of these virtues as real and enduring wealth.

This means that the connection between work and (financial) wealth is not necessarily causal. What I mean here is that we must not value the work that someone does by the quantity of money that it generates. A woman that gives herself selflessly to missionary work or to caring for a family or an elderly relative will not generate a substantial financial reward but she will generate a wealth of character and experience that no money could buy.

Once we know the difference between the goal of work and its rewards, the next thing to think about is how we can deploy those rewards in order to help us reach the goal of seeking the Kingdom of God. From the very beginning, the wealth generated by work, has been used to further the kingdom of God through the spread of the gospel, and so it has been ever since. We have just looked at one example of this: the collection for the relief of poor believers in Jerusalem. More generally, giving to the poor, whether believers or not, has always been a part of the way in which Christians have expressed their faith, and most people, whether Christians or not, can see the importance and value of such charitable work.

However, what non-Christians find hard to understand and, indeed, many Christians do not take as seriously as they should, is giving that is directed towards supporting the work of spreading the gospel, in obedience to the Great Commission. Yet such a gospel focus for the use of wealth was evident from the very beginning.

For Luke tells us, how the itinerant ministry of Jesus and His disciples, was supported by a group of women who travelled with them: 'Soon afterward he went on through cities and villages, proclaiming and bringing the good news of the kingdom of God. And the twelve were with him, and also some women who had been healed of evil spirits and infirmities: Mary, called Magdalene, from whom seven demons had gone out, and Joanna, the wife of Chuza, Herod's household manager, and Susanna, and many others, who provided for them out of their means' (Luke 8:1-3).

Some of these women, like Joanna, were probably from well-to-do families; others like Mary were not, but they contributed what they could. They all contributed that most precious commodity of all – time. It was a vital, though costly ministry.

In the book of Acts, the first history of the Christian church, Luke tells us that some churches met in homes. Clearly, then, there were believers who owned homes that were big enough to accommodate a fair number of people. We read of Priscilla and Aquila using their home to help Apollos. Luke also tells of the conversion of an international fabric merchant, Lydia, from Thyatira, who was on a business visit to Philippi. She became a Christian after listening to Paul – apparently the very first convert in Europe. She immediately and imaginatively saw the potential of her wealth – she could use it to provide a base for Paul and his team in her home (Acts 16:13-15).

These examples introduce us to the idea of gospel patronage, which we may think of as the combination of different kinds of wealth in order to spread the gospel effectively. Paul and his team were gifted with spiritual and intellectual wealth, Lydia with financial wealth, and the combination of the two, with Lydia as Paul's team's patron, was strategic in establishing a bridgehead for the gospel in Europe – to which many of us, including myself, are, and will be eternally indebted. It is not hard to see that such deep and costly commitment to the spread of the gospel, led to enduring relationships between those involved – serving together, using their varied abilities, and wealth, for the common aim of extending the kingdom of God. Thus, from the beginning, gospel patronage was characterised by the spread of the gospel, by communicating the message of the Word in a relational and sacrificial way.

Now the danger with using the word 'patron' is that it is often used for someone who is very wealthy, and there certainly are some remarkable stories of the way in which very rich people have been used to spread the gospel. These accounts deserve to be better-known than they are, since they show how God is at work at all levels of society. True, as Paul says, there are not many rich – but there are some.

For instance, there was an evangelical awakening in Russia in the late nineteenth century,[1] when a certain wealthy nobleman, Count Pashkov, got converted through Lord Radstock, a believer from the UK, who had been invited to visit St Petersburg in the 1870s by women from the Russian nobility. These women opened their homes for him to preach, and it was in this way that the gospel penetrated deeply into the high society of the then Russian capital.

During Radstock's six-month stay in St Petersburg, he regularly preached in the salons of the aristocrats with the result that a number of the Russian élite became believers. In

---

[1] Major reference is Edmund Heier's *Religious Schism and the Russian Aristocracy, 1860-1900: Radstockism and Pashkovism* [157 pp, Martinus Hijhoff, The Hague, 1970].
 See also https://repository.up.ac.za/bitstream/handle/2263/26868/03chapter4.pdf?sequence=4&isAllowed=y

this way, after he left, there were a group of capable people to carry on such meetings. To that group, there belonged Colonel Pashkov, Count Korff, Count Bobrinsky, Princess Natalie Lieven, and her sister Princess Vera Gagarina. For decades, meetings were held right in the Lieven and Gagarina palaces that stood next to each other in Morskaya Street, in St Petersburg. Lieven's daughter Sophie recalled: 'Our guests often admired our house and my mother used to tell them, "This house belongs to the Lord; I am nothing but Christ's servant."'

The palace at Bolshaya Morskaya 43 functioned, not only as a church but also as a hotel for preachers. Princess Lieven repeatedly invited Radstock, Baedeker, Müller, and others to stay with her family as guests. She also hosted a six-week Bible course for young preachers. Her palace was the centre of evangelical meetings for over thirty years, long after the first leaders of the movement had been exiled by the authorities. Indeed, she herself assumed leadership of the meetings held in her palace after Pashkov and Korff's banishment from Russia in 1884. Inevitably, the authorities told her to stop the meetings under threat of exile, and reported to the Tsar, Alexander III. Her famous response was: 'Ask His Majesty whom I have to obey, God or Emperor?' Alexander III is said to have replied: 'She is a widow; leave her in peace.' As a result, the meetings in her home continued for many more years, until around 1912.

It is important to note that these high-born people did not restrict their message to their own class, but rather used their large homes and ballrooms to bring all kinds of people in, so that the gospel message spread rapidly in a remarkable top-down chain. It was a superb example of gospel patronage.

What needs to be emphasised here, however, is that, once the gospel fire had been lit, it was carried throughout the country by ordinary, humble believers, many of whom were very poor.

When, many years ago, I first came across the account of this revival in Russia, I little realised that one day I, too, would be privileged to carry the message to Russia once more – this time to the Academies of Science, Universities,

Colleges and Schools – and to publish books (some of which were co-authored with my mentor David Gooding). They were distributed in hundreds of thousands, mainly to school children, thanks to wonderful gospel patronage from many sources, both small and great.

Luke was a doctor, and used his wealth of medical knowledge to support Paul and his team on some of their missionary journeys, as they travelled through areas where there was considerable risk of disease and danger. Paul called him the 'beloved physician'.

Luke was also a historian, and we owe to him the existence of the two volume work, Luke and Acts. Those books were dedicated to the honourable Theophilus, who, in all likelihood, commissioned and funded Luke to do the research, and write-up the historical accounts. Luke's wealth of intellect, and Theophilus' financial wealth, combined to give us a large part of the New Testament. Money alone could not have done it.

Not only the original writing of Scripture, but its translation for the masses, has depended on patronage of this kind. One of the most famous examples from the sixteenth century is William Tyndale's prodigious work in translating the New Testament. He was turned down by the Bishop of London, who was not prepared to support this venture. In 1523, a brave and far-sighted Christian cloth merchant and trader, Humphrey Monmouth, partnered with Tyndale and became his patron, funding Tyndale's mission to translate the Scriptures into English, thus making them available to the common man. Monmouth took great risks smuggling Tyndale's Bibles into England in his ships. He was incarcerated in the Tower of London for a whole year for his support for Tyndale, and Luther.

John Rinehart, in his informative book, Gospel Patrons,[2] relates the story of Monmouth and Tyndale in more detail. He also tells how later, in the eighteenth century, Lady Huntingdon invited members of her aristocratic circle into her London home, to hear George Whitefield preach the gospel.

All of us, therefore, are deeply indebted to gospel patrons in the past, and many Christians today would testify that

---

[2] Reclaimed Publishing, Minneapolis, 2013

they could not have done what they have done without the investment of others who believed in, prayed for and supported them. Ultimately, of course, all wealth comes from the Lord. It comes in various forms: there is wealth of personal endowment – physical, emotional, intellectual, spiritual, artistic, musical, financial wealth, wealth of organisational and negotiating skills and business acumen, wealth of wisdom and insight, wealth of character, friendliness, and contentment.

We should, therefore, resist the cultural tendency to think of all wealth as financial. A person's 'net worth' is usually calculated in terms of cash, but what about net worth in terms of moral integrity, as a husband or wife, a father, a friend, as a business person, or as a doctor, or historian like Luke? A person could have a monetary net worth of billions, but a net moral worth of zero as a husband and father, if he selfishly deserts his wife and family.

We see, both in the book of Acts, and throughout subsequent history, the way in which the Lord furthers the message of His kingdom, by combining teams of people having different kinds of wealth: for instance, the intellectual wealth of Luke as a historian, and the apostolic gift given to Paul, the financial wealth of Humphrey Monmouth, and the linguistic and intellectual wealth of Tyndale. In a much lesser way, I have experienced this personally, and I think it is worth spelling this out, since I sense an objection arising in some of my readers' minds that would run something like this: Look, I am a businessman who knows how the commercial world operates, and who has made a great deal of money. You, on the other hand, are an academic who lived on a university salary (a pension now!). Therefore, what right have you to tell me what to do with my wealth, since you have no idea of the decisions I have to face.

Well, prioritizing the distribution of whatever wealth we have is an intensely personal matter, and most of us, including me, find it difficult. And you are right, telling others how to set those priorities is none of my business. Indeed, the last thing I would wish to do is to tell you what to do with your wealth: that is the Lord's prerogative, not mine, and it is very important that both of us recognise that. We each must make our decisions before the Lord as to what we do. That will involve constant observing where real needs are: learning to distinguish them from spurious appeals for help; getting to know people we can trust; working out what we should give to charity in general; and what should be earmarked for gospel outreach at home and abroad. That is why having connections is in itself wealth, since there are many people with wealth of various kinds, but they are not connected with those who can help them place that wealth, in order to further the spread of the gospel. Many financially wealthy people would love to give to gospel causes, but they don't have the connections to do so in a way that gives them some certainty that they are supporting something worthwhile. Putting one kind of wealth in touch with another is itself a vital gift.

As to your objection to my saying anything on the topic, that could be of relevance to you, yes. I understand that you may think that academics like myself are impractical theorists! However, if you will allow me to explain, you may just find that I understand the issues a bit better than you think. In order to do that, I need to talk a little about my own journey, and the grace and goodness of God that I have experienced.

It gradually dawned on me at school that I had been blessed by the Lord with considerable intellectual wealth. Just like those believers like yourself with financial wealth – though you may not have received it, as a teenager I had increasingly to make decisions as to how to invest my kind of wealth. Various possibilities presented themselves. I had become increasingly interested, not only in my school subjects, but also in Scripture: not only in understanding it, but communicating it, and, even in my late teens, I occasionally gave short talks in a church context.

I was particularly inspired to do this after meeting a classics professor, David Gooding, who opened my eyes to the riches of the Bible, and invested a lot of his time in showing me how to find them for myself. He eventually became a lifelong mentor, colleague, friend and co-author.

As a result of that input and my own building on its capital, I increasingly found myself being invited to lead Bible studies and teach the Bible in churches and at Christian conferences.

During this time, I was studying at Cambridge, first for my undergraduate degree and then for my PhD. I got married in my last year at university in 1968, and the following year got a lectureship in mathematics in the University of Wales in Cardiff.

I was now responsible for a wife, lecturing, research, and administration in a mathematics department. I felt responsible as a young husband to provide for my wife and family, and to do my work with integrity and commitment. I also felt a strong inner call to teach the Bible. That meant that I had to invest a great deal of time, both in Bible study and also in speaking in many small churches up and down the Welsh valleys, that radiated inland from Cardiff. One implication was that I was not often able to engage in mathematical research at home in the evenings, to the extent that some of my colleagues did, although marking had to be done, as it usually could not wait.

I made up my mind that I would work conscientiously unto the Lord, but that I would not sell my soul for my work, as many seemed to do, not only in the world of academia, but also in business.

My decision also meant that my wife had to sacrifice time with me, although in the early days, she often travelled with me in the evenings, and at weekends, to local speaking engagements, and sometimes to residential conferences. Over the years she has given tremendous and costly support to my Bible-teaching activities. In time, we had children, three in total, and the problem of juggling commitment priorities, inevitably increased.

As a family of four (before our third child was born), we spent the academic year of 1975-76 in West Germany. At the end of that year, a Hungarian Christian I met in Berlin, unexpectedly invited me to give some Bible talks in Hungary, the following year. It was the beginning of a new direction in my life: that of international travel, mainly to speak at Bible-teaching conferences, sometimes combined with mathematics conferences – and usually combined with doing mathematical research in the daytime, with the preaching done in the evenings.

I was now faced with a new and very practical problem: travel and hotel costs. The countries to which I travelled at the time were mostly behind the Iron Curtain. The believers there were in no position to fund travel costs, to say nothing of the cost of staying in hotels, which was the only option in those days, in order to protect the Christians that I was visiting.

As a result of an error (which was not corrected for many years) my university salary was lower than it should have been. In consequence, in order to provide for my family, I had to take on extra work translating mathematical papers from Russian to English. This activity was exacting, and not well-paid, but was the only way open to me to make slightly more money. I little realised that the knowledge of Russian gained through doing it would one day become very important and useful to me.

The upshot of all of this was that I was in no position to fund trips to countries in the Communist Block to which I had been invited.

As a young person I had read about George Müller, the founder of Müller's Children's Homes and so I knew how he quietly trusted the Lord to supply his (considerable) needs without making them publicly known. I decided to do the same, as I really wished to be sure that this calling really was from God, as it involved major investment of my time in study and preparation, and time away from home and family, when my wife would have to cope with the children on her own. And what about the mathematics; could I do that abroad as well?

What happened was my first experience of gospel patronage. A Christian businessman contacted me, and told me that he had heard about my activities (not from me), and that he wished to fund my travel and hotel expenses. He was faithful to his word, and generously did so for many years. There were years when I probably travelled nearly as much as all my colleagues in the mathematics department put together, since we had very few resources for external visits.

My patron's financial wealth enabled me to use my wealth of understanding Scriptures, such as it was, to invest in many people who were thirsty for the word of God, to an extent that

I had never before experienced. By giving to the Lord's work through me, my patron was, of course, by definition, reducing the amount of fluid cash for his business. He was, however, laying up treasure in heaven.

It is important to say that receiving such patronage did not relieve me of the responsibility to share my own financial resources. We all have multiple kinds of wealth, and the Lord has delegated to us the responsibility of deciding how to invest it as stewards in His kingdom.

Over the years I have had the joy of experiencing patronage that has greatly extended the reach of my ministry. For instance, I am ultimately greatly indebted to the late Sir John Laing, who was famous for making God 'his partner' in his construction business, on an occasion when one of his major projects was in serious trouble. He carried out his commitment, and the charitable trusts, that bear his name, have made a huge impact on Christian work around the world: in particular, in facilitating missionary work, evangelism and student work, such as UCCF and IFES, and theological education (e.g. London School of Theology). I have benefitted for the past 25 years from the support of the J W Laing Trust, as the Laing Trust Fellow at Green Templeton College (formerly Green College), in Oxford. Laing's story deserves to be known much more widely and the centenary of the foundation of the J W Laing Trust was celebrated in October 2022, the occasion being marked by the production of a short film about Sir John's life and influence and by a new and authoritative book on the history of the Trust written by its former Chairman, Alex McIlhenny in which he records a memorable statement by Sir John: 'Business has a tendency to make a man mercenary, which the service of giving counteracts.'[3]

Another example is that I was approached by an American Christian businessman and inventor. He had read one of my books, and it resonated so much with his thinking, that he wished to do something to get my thoughts and ideas out to a wider public. His idea was to make a film. The documentary, *Against the Tide*, featuring myself and Kevin Sorbo, has now

---

[3]   *The Service of Giving*, (Darvel, Opal Trust 2022).

been released. Its production in the end involved several generous patrons, who saw the potential and decided to help.

As I think about the patronage I have experienced over the years, I am acutely aware of how so much of what I have been able to do would never have been done without it. I am deeply grateful.

A final word on this. We should not let the rather grandiose-sounding title, gospel patron, obscure the fact that all believers can – and many, if not most, do – support Christian work; and are therefore involved as gospel patrons, even though they might not think of themselves as such. After all, it is easy to be overwhelmed by the vast riches of a Humphrey Monmouth, a Lady Huntingdon, a Count Pashkov, or a Princess Lieven, and feel that, by comparison, we are contributing nothing.

However, that is not so. Luke, whose patron was Theophilus, was himself interested in the matter of support for the gospel on the part of people, who may have felt that what they did was insignificant, for the obvious reason that they were very poor. The most famous example is Jesus' comment on people putting money in a collection box: 'Jesus looked up and saw the rich putting their gifts into the offering box, and he saw a poor widow put in two small copper coins. And he said, "Truly, I tell you, this poor widow has put in more than all of them. For they all contributed out of their abundance, but she out of her poverty put in all she had to live on"' (Luke 21:1-4).

Once again the lesson here is the important one that we mentioned earlier but which is worth emphasising once more, that the connection between work and financial wealth is not necessarily causal.

It is the sobering truth that God does not measure our financial contributions to His work in terms of quantity, but quality. Perhaps this was one of the reasons that, regarding charitable giving, Jesus said:

> Beware of practising your righteousness before other people in order to be seen by them, for then you will have no reward from your Father who is in heaven. Thus, when you give to the needy, sound no trumpet before you, as the hypocrites do in the synagogues and in the streets, that they may be praised by others. Truly, I say to you, they have received their reward. But

when you give to the needy, do not let your left hand know what your right hand is doing, so that your giving may be in secret. And your Father who sees in secret will reward you. (Matt. 6:1-4)

The human heart is such that, if we are not careful, we can do our giving, yes, even to gospel work, with the motivation of attracting peoples' attention to what we think is the impressive extent of our generosity. Jesus points out that others' attention and praise is all we shall get, as there will be no response from God the Father in heaven, who is not impressed in the slightest. As a result, there will be many surprises in the day when the Lord rewards the faithful – the secret, unnoticed small-scale giving of humble believers will become jewels in their crowns, whereas some vast benefaction, done ostentatiously, will not even get a mention. Let us never give the impression that it is the amount that counts. The elite of heaven will not necessarily be the elite of earth.

It is worth constantly reminding ourselves that the gospel starts with the generous patronage of God the Father Himself: 'What do you have that you did not receive?' (1 Cor. 4:7) says Paul. The answer is: nothing – and that at every level. Yes, God has given, and the question for us is: what do we do with what He has given? How do we manage the manifold gifts that we have received?

Questions

1. What is a gospel patron in your view? Why is Gospel patronage important?
2. Do you have to be very wealthy to be a gospel patron?
3. What examples in this chapter do you find speaking to you, and why?
4. Ask yourself how you might be a gospel patron, if you are in a position to be one?

CHAPTER 6

WEALTH MANAGEMENT

A cursory glance at the Gospels shows that Luke is very interested in attitudes to the material possessions of both rich and poor. We have already seen how he tells us of the support that Jesus and the disciples received from certain well-to-do women. We have also thought about the widow's mite.

We shall base our further discussion mainly on Luke's record of what Jesus said about wealth management. This teaching circles around several of Jesus' most famous parables, including the Rich Fool, the Lost Son, the Dishonest Steward, and the (unnamed) Rich Man, and Lazarus, the Poor Man.[1]

THE RICH FOOL (LUKE 12:13-21)

A huge crowd numbering thousands had gathered around Jesus. Some were hostile, and He warned His disciples that persecution awaited them. In the midst of all this, a man came up to Jesus and asked Him to intervene in a family dispute.

Luke tells us how the situation developed:

---

[1]   I am indebted here to Kenneth Bailey's book: *Jesus through Middle Eastern Eyes*, (London, SPCK, 2008).

> Someone in the crowd said to him, 'Teacher, tell my brother to divide the inheritance with me.' But he said to him, 'Man, who made me a judge or arbitrator over you?' And he said to them, 'Take care, and be on your guard against all covetousness, for one's life does not consist in the abundance of his possessions.' And he told them a parable, saying, 'The land of a rich man produced plentifully, and he thought to himself, 'What shall I do, for I have nowhere to store my crops?' And he said, 'I will do this: I will tear down my barns and build larger ones, and there I will store all my grain and my goods. And I will say to my soul, Soul, you have ample goods laid up for many years; relax, eat, drink, be merry.' But God said to him, 'Fool! This night your soul is required of you, and the things you have prepared, whose will they be?' So is the one who lays up treasure for himself and is not rich towards God.

We do not know whether the man had a fair case or not, since Jesus refused to adjudicate. He clearly did not consider it His responsibility to do so at that time, although He will do such things at His return, as we shall later see. What Jesus takes the opportunity to do, is to issue a warning to the crowd against the danger of all kinds of covetousness – and it is not hard to see why in that context.

David Gooding's comment is apt:

> When it comes to material possessions Christ does not hold that getting our legal rights is necessarily the best thing for us to do. It is possible (though not necessary) that in going for our legal rights in the matter of possessions, we could be (sometimes, though not always) motivated by covetousness. In which case, getting our legal rights would be a victory for our covetousness. Christ will never help us to achieve such a "victory".[2]

Gooding goes on to explain that the Greek word for covetousness, *pleonexia*, means 'having, or wanting to have, more (more, that is, than one's fair share)'. The reason Jesus gives for warning against it is that 'one's life does not consist in the abundance of one's possessions'. Gooding points out that the Greek word for *abundance* in this context does not

---

[2]   *According to Luke*, (Belfast, Myrtlefield House, 2013), p.251.

simply mean *plentiful,* but *excess* in the sense of having more than enough.[3] So, Jesus is not saying that a reasonable supply of goods in this life is either wrong or unnecessary: He is saying that, although we need enough goods in order to live, life does not consist in what we possess, over and above what is necessary to meet our needs.

Jesus now tells a parable to illustrate what this means in everyday life, in an agricultural community. A wealthy farmer has had a successful harvest and has far more than he needs. The Greek word in verse 16, translated *plentifully,* is the word *euphoria.* That tells us exactly how he felt – euphoric. He decides to take the pretty extreme measure of pulling down his existing barns and building even bigger ones to store his bumper harvest. He contemplates a long, trouble-free retirement.

God calls him a fool. He has made several false assumptions. Firstly, that his wealth is only for himself and his pleasure; secondly that he has many years to live, when in fact he has less than twenty-four hours left so that, thirdly, he has failed to take on board the fact that he is mortal. When he dies, all his goods will pass to someone else, and he will never enjoy them personally. He has not been rich towards God – indeed he has not thought about God at all, which is the most foolish thing anyone can do.

James repeats this teaching on the danger of procrastination:

> Come now, you who say, 'Today or tomorrow we will go into such and such a town and spend a year there and trade and make a profit' – yet you do not know what tomorrow will bring. What is your life? For you are a mist that appears for a little time and then vanishes. Instead, you ought to say, 'If the Lord wills, we will live and do this or that.' As it is, you boast in your arrogance. All such boasting is evil. So whoever knows the right thing to do and fails to do it, for him it is sin. (Jas. 4:13-17)

The lesson is plain: both our physical life and our goods, are God's gifts to us. He can take back our life at any time – a fact that it is foolish to ignore. Life has an eternal dimension, and

---

3   The word is also used with the same meaning in Luke 9:17 of 'the fragments that *remained over* '(RV), and in 15:17 of 'food *enough and to spare*'.

therefore we need to make our plans for the future, in light of the fact that we might find ourselves in eternity, much sooner than we expected. Moses taught this to the people of Israel in a passage from Deuteronomy, that should be read in its entirety:

> Take care lest you forget the Lord your God by not keeping his commandments and his rules and his statutes, which I command you today, lest, when you have eaten and are full and have built good houses and live in them, and when your herds and flocks multiply and your silver and gold is multiplied and all that you have is multiplied, then your heart be lifted up, and you forget the Lord your God, who brought you out of the land of Egypt, out of the house of slavery, who led you through the great and terrifying wilderness, with its fiery serpents and scorpions and thirsty ground where there was no water, who brought you water out of the flinty rock, who fed you in the wilderness with manna that your fathers did not know, that he might humble you and test you, to do you good in the end. Beware lest you say in your heart, 'My power and the might of my hand have gained me this wealth.' You shall remember the Lord your God, for it is he who gives you power to get wealth, that he may confirm his covenant that he swore to your fathers, as it is this day. And if you forget the Lord your God and go after other gods and serve them and worship them, I solemnly warn you today that you shall surely perish. Like the nations that the Lord makes to perish before you, so shall you perish, because you would not obey the voice of the Lord your God. (Deut. 8:11-20)

Centuries before Jesus told the parable of the Rich Fool, God warned the people of the danger of the attitude he showed – note verse 17 in particular, in James 4.

We need, therefore, to be wise in the way we use our material goods to ensure that, as Jesus said, we are being rich towards God by investing them to please Him and promote godliness. But what will that involve?

Covetousness centres on the human heart, and its desire for something it hasn't got. Who among us will claim never to have felt this strong desire for more to add to our treasure – our store of the stuff that we consider valuable?

Just after the parable on the Rich Fool, Luke picks up Jesus' teaching about seeking the kingdom of God in our work, that we discussed in Chapters 2 and 3. We strongly recommend Gooding's account of it, to the reader looking for a larger perspective.

THE PARABLE OF THE LOST SON (Luke 15:11–32)

This story details an extreme form of patronage abuse, in which a son demands his inheritance before his father dies. His demand implies that he wishes his father dead, an attitude that would be regarded as shocking in a Middle Eastern setting. Jesus' listeners would be aghast to hear such a thing.

Jesus continues to relate that the father, nevertheless, gives the son his allocated portion of the inheritance and, perhaps not so surprisingly, the son proceeds to waste it on extravagance and frivolity. When, inevitably, his money runs out, he loses all his fair-weather 'friends'. He is reduced to taking a job as a swineherd in a world where there is no giving of any kind, let alone the kind of generosity he had experienced from his father. He is not even offered the pigswill, even though he was so desperate that he would have eaten it, if it had been offered.

This leads to a crisis moment of truth. His eyes are opened in the pigsty. The starving, disillusioned man recalls his home, with all its comforts: food, security, and potential for well-being. He realises that he has been an utter fool in throwing away the place where he belongs – at home. He undergoes a thorough change of heart, repents and decides to return and throw himself on his father's mercy. He has no expectation of being reinstated as a son with all his earlier privileges. He thinks, however, that there might just be a chance of his becoming a lowly hired hand on his father's estate. To his utter surprise, on his return to the village, he is met with amazing grace: his father runs to meet him, not something dignified senior men did in those days. The father welcomes his long-lost son with open arms, and celebrates his homecoming with a lavish party. It is a wonderful illustration of the heart of the Christian message: opening your eyes to the truth, recognising the need to go home to the Father, repenting and going home.

When he gets home his elder brother objects, because he does not understand the father's generous heart. Why should his waster of a brother be given a party, when he was never given one, even though he had stayed at home?

The main lessons are clear:

1. God is prepared to receive us even if we have squandered His gifts, provided we repent and return to Him.

2. There are people like the elder brother – the Pharisees mentioned in the context – who claim to be faithful to God, but who think the gospel of unmerited forgiveness is wasteful, and even immoral. They have never grasped what grace means.

3. The son wasted his father's goods and broke his father's trust in him. Yet the father took him back. Thousands of people have been converted listening to this parable, as the wonder of the grace of God has dawned on them. God is prepared to forgive anyone who genuinely repents, even if he or she has made a mess of their lives.

4. That raises an obvious question. Suppose we have frittered away what God has given us, does that really matter, if, in the end, we repent and return to the Lord? Is that what the parable is teaching us? No, it is not, and, in order to see why, and avoid any misunderstanding, Jesus now tells another parable about someone else, who was accused of wasting goods that were not his own.

THE PARABLE OF THE DISHONEST MANAGER
(Luke 16:1-13)

The word for manager, or steward, is the Greek *oikonomos*, from which we get our word *economics*. It means *the law of the house* (*oikos = house, nomos = law*) and was used to designate either a banker's agent, or the manager of a farm. The latter is probably the case here, judging from the nature of the debts mentioned.

This manager was accused to his wealthy boss of being a waster. Charges (plural) were brought. That tells us that those who brought the accusations expected the boss to do something about them, which in turn implies, in that Middle Eastern context, that the boss was respected in the community. If he had been regarded as a scoundrel, no one would have bothered telling him about the steward. 'Serves him right,' they would say. Also, the boss clearly regarded the sources of the accusation as reliable, as he acts on them, and summons the manager to account: 'What is this that I hear about you?' Is the boss asking for information? Not really. He wants to see the reaction of the manager. If the manager panics, he might reveal a lot more about what has been going on. However, he does not appear to say anything. The tension of silence in the narrative is broken by the rich man telling the manager to turn in the books (not to balance them). In effect: 'You're fired!'

In ancient law, such a firing was regarded as taking instant effect, so that what the manager proceeds to do is illegal, but it is no longer the boss's responsibility. Handing in the books means the cessation of the manager's authority over the estate, that is, when he does hand them in, for he still has them. The rest of the story turns on that circumstance.

Now comes the astonishing thing in the narrative. There is no mention of the manager asking to be reinstated. Kenneth Bailey, mentioned above, spent decades observing the Middle Eastern scene, says that he never once came across a situation where a dismissed manager did not plead to be reinstated. Many arguments were used to do that: 1. My father worked for you, and so did my grandfather, how can you let me go? 2. Who are the people that accused me? Bring them here and let me confront them, for they are nothing but liars. 3. It wasn't my fault. We have been so busy that some of the work got a bit sloppy, but surely you are big enough to let it go just this once, please … etc., etc.

There was no such protest here, which means that the manager knows that protest would be of no use. His boss was a man of integrity, who would not budge on such an issue.

As the manager now goes to get the account books, he talks to himself and surveys the range of his possibilities. He must get work. Manual labour? Not strong enough. Begging? Ashamed to do it. Not everyone in such a situation would be ashamed to beg, so we have here an indication that the manager possesses some residual sense of personal dignity.

Then, a possible solution dawns on him. He can see a way of doing something that could lead to him being 'received into another house', which is a phrase meaning 'being offered another job', according to the first-century Greek Stoic philosopher Epictetus. The manager knows that, if it ever leaks out that he was fired for fraud, he will never get employment again. He cooks up a clever scheme that will do two things: demonstrate his shrewdness and, at the same time and very importantly for his future, make him popular, maybe even employable.

He now makes haste to use the brief time window, during which noone, except himself and his boss, know that he has been fired. He summons some of the debtors (presumably those who rent land from the rich man) to come to him individually. He asks the first: how much do you owe? He is not asking for information, as he already has the rental agreement in front of him. He is initiating negotiations, by getting the debtors agreement on the amount owed. If the amount on the steward's docket agrees with what the debtor says, they can proceed to the next stage. If not, there will have to be some haggling.

The first debtor admits that he owes 100 measures of olive oil, whereupon the manager reaches him his docket, and tells him to sit down and write 50. This is an enormous reduction, since 50 measures of oil, at that time, were worth around 500 denarii – a year's wages for a farm labourer. Note that the manager gets the debtor to write the change on the docket, so that anyone looking at the accounts will know that the debtor has been involved in the transaction and, therefore, knows all about it.

Thus, having been fired for stealing, the manager decides that his best course of action is to steal a great deal more!

The Arab commentator, Ibn al-Tayyib, points out that this parable is set in an honour-shame culture, that makes a clear distinction between public propriety and private awareness. Public propriety preserves personal honour. In this case, the debtor's public stance will be that he didn't know that the steward had been fired, and so naturally thought that the reduction had been authorised by the boss. Privately, the debtor will accept a little deal that benefits both himself and the steward, since the manager's instruction to 'sit down and write 50', implies that the extra 50 will be split between the two of them afterwards. By being complicit, the debtor has forfeited the possibility of going to the boss later, and telling him what really happened. Clever stuff! I hope this is not giving anyone ideas!

The upshot is not hard to predict. Having received such generous rebates, the delighted debtors will go home and tell their families and friends the great news of their debt relief. That news will spread like wildfire around the village, until the whole community is celebrating the generosity of the rich man.

The steward returns the books and makes himself scarce. It will not be long until the boss finds out the fraud that has been perpetrated by the wily, thieving manager. But what is he now going to do about it? Indeed, what can he do about it? If he goes back to the debtors, and informs them that they have completely misread the situation, since fraud has taken place, and the debts have not been altered as they think, the festivities will cease at once, and the rich man will now be the subject of endless vilification.

His only real alternative is to dig deep into his generosity, take the hit, and enjoy his heightened celebrity. We should note that the fact that he simply fires the steward, is another mark of his magnanimity: after all, he could have had him imprisoned, or sold into slavery, possibly with his family as well.

As for the sacked manager, he is likely to get a job again, since the locals will take the view, better have him working for us than against us, since he did, after all, save us a lot of money, and might do so again – but he will be carefully watched.

The narrative now tells us that the boss (not the Lord Jesus, please note) commends the manager for his shrewdness, but not, of course, for his dishonesty. You can just imagine him saying: 'You clever old so-and-so. How did you ever think of that?'

It is a fascinating parable, brilliantly designed to light up Jesus' audience. He now applies it, and it is important to notice the precise terms in which He does so. He applies it to His disciples, who are 'sons of light'; which the manager most assuredly was not. He was a dishonest man, a son of darkness. Yet the sons of light, believers in God, that is, can learn something very important from the man's shrewdness.

We need to get this straight. In Jesus' application, it is not the disciples who are unrighteous – it is money that is unrighteous, hence the description 'unrighteous wealth'. This is a strange phrase, at first sight. Yet it is not hard to see what it might mean.

We all know that evil in society has resulted in an uneven and unfair distribution of wealth: where a nurse, driven to exhaustion, putting her life at risk, fighting a pandemic, earns a fraction of a top footballer, or a person in any number of professions where there is no risk to life. Such unfairness and injustice is so deeply embedded in the structures of our culture, that it is hard to imagine that it will ever be put right, granted what human nature is like.

Jesus recognises this, and so tells us to act as honest managers, and use what we have righteously, even though it may be tainted at levels of which we are not even aware. Think of a believer with a high-powered job in a major automobile industry, who does not know that some of the wealth she enjoys is due to the fact that some engineers have manipulated the emissions in the cars to give false readings, resulting in them selling well, and producing vast revenues for her employers.

From God's perspective, that wealth is tainted. Is she herself, therefore, complicit in evil? If she donates some of her salary for medical missionary work, are the grateful recipients also cooperating with evil? Or, is what is going on here, a carrying out of what Jesus says?

Putting it another way, most wealth tends to be tainted somewhere along the line; much of it is beyond our ability even to know about, let alone change. This passage would seem to be telling us that the Lord recognises this circumstance, and therefore does not put the accent on us, trying to sort it out, but emphasises what we, as righteous 'managers' this time, should actually do with our 'unrighteous wealth'?

We may not have been fired like the dishonest manager, but we need to realise that we are temporarily here in this world. We therefore only have influence for a limited time before we leave this world at an unspecified date in the future. That day may come sooner than we think: remember the rich fool and his unexpectedly sudden demise. Jesus says that while we are here, we are to use what we have, in order to *make friends*. What sort of friends? Not the kind that the dishonest manager made, who connived at his fraud, and so participated in his dishonesty. Nor like those fair-weather 'friends' of the runaway son in the preceding parable, who left him as soon as the money supply dried up.

Jesus tells His disciples, and through them believers all down through the ages, that they are to make the kind of friends that *'will receive you into eternal tabernacles'* (Luke 16:9). That is, friends who become, or are, believers, and who go to heaven to be with the Lord, before we do. They will receive us on our arrival.

I suspect that this is all somewhat unfamiliar territory to many of us, and so it needs some teasing out to get at its implications, and they are both considerable and important. The first thing to see is that this is not a matter of a mercenary 'buying' friends, as the prodigal son did. It is doing something with our possessions, that has the effect of increasing our circle of friends in eternity, friends that we may be mostly unaware about.

Remember Humphrey Monmouth, who financed Tyndale's translation of the Bible into English. I like to think about what will happen one day. Along with all of us (see later) Humphrey Monmouth will arrive at the judgement seat of Christ in heaven. Can you imagine how the untold multitudes of people who were converted through Tyndale's translation will react as they learn that it was Monmouth's money, and Tyndale's hard work, that were instrumental under God in their conversion? They will receive those two men as friends, will they not? The same will be true of the thousands converted through the preaching of George Whitefield and John Newton, when they meet Lady Huntingdon and John Thornton.

Humphrey Monmouth, Lady Huntingdon, John Thornton, and thousands of other patrons who did their work behind the scenes, have laid up a good foundation for the world to come.

This will not only happen to wealthy patrons. At a much humbler level, think of a medical student who arrived at her Cambridge college, and was feeling quite lonely in her college room when a knock came at the door. It was a fellow student asking if she would like to join her for coffee. They chatted and eventually, the first student asked the second, why she had invited her. It was not long before the student who provided the coffee was quietly talking about her Christian faith. Not long after that, the medical student gave her life to Christ. I don't know who the student who shared her faith was, but many hundreds of thousands know who the medical student was – Helen Roseveare.

Just think about it. The first student shared her coffee. Coffee costs money, and she could have kept it all to herself. But she decided to use it to express friendship in a natural way. She had no idea of what would flow from that encounter – and yet it turned out to be a wonderful example of gospel patronage. Just imagine the reaction of the thousands of Africans who became believers through Helen Roseveare's ministry. They were Helen's friends, but won't the girl who gave Helen the coffee be instantly received as their friend too? She will have a vast circle of friends in the world to come.

The parable of the dishonest manager is about money. Yet, it is clear that the principles that Jesus used the parable to teach apply to all those other kinds of wealth we have mentioned earlier. Indeed, the student used not only her money, but gave her time to befriending Helen Roseveare.

One of the main, very encouraging lessons here, is that this is open to anyone. It was, after all, only a cup of coffee! What an illustration of the potential of small things. After all, a young man's five loaves and two fish were used by the Lord to feed five thousand people. The key was to put them into the Lord's hands. ...

Thus far, Jesus' parables have taught us (among other things):

1. God's grace is such that He is prepared to receive a repentant prodigal at the eleventh hour, even though he has wasted what he had been given.
2. However, it does matter and matter eternally if we waste what we have been given. We have a responsibility to use the by-products of work to make friends that will be in heaven to welcome us.

Paul enunciates a similar principle for wealthy believers:

> 'As for the rich in this present age, charge them not to be haughty, nor to set their hopes on the uncertainty of riches, but on God, who richly provides us with everything to enjoy. They are to do good, to be rich in good works, to be generous and ready to share, thus storing up treasure for themselves as a good foundation for the future, so that they may take hold of that which is truly life.' (1 Tim. 6:17-19)

We notice that Paul says that those who are rich in *this present age* will only be rich in the future if they invest in God's kingdom in this life, and lay up a good foundation for *the future*. That is the only sensible investment strategy.

There is more to be said. In particular, what about those people who are not rich in this age? It is all very well telling believers to *'make to yourselves friends of the mammon of unrighteousness'* (Luke 16:9 KJV), but what happens if they don't have any resources to do that? In order to answer that question, Jesus now tells another story about someone in just that situation. I use the word 'story' rather than 'parable', since the account reads like a story about actual people, which is confirmed by the use of a personal name, Lazarus, a feature that appears in no other parable that Jesus told. The fact that the rich man is not also named, may show the relative importance of the two characters.

THE RICH MAN AND LAZARUS (Luke 16:19-26)

> There was a rich man who was clothed in purple and fine linen and who feasted sumptuously every day. And at his gate was laid a poor man named Lazarus, covered with sores, who desired to be fed with what fell from the rich man's table. Moreover, even the dogs came and licked his sores. The poor man died

and was carried by the angels to Abraham's side. The rich man also died and was buried, and in Hades, being in torment, he lifted up his eyes and saw Abraham far off and Lazarus at his side. And he called out, 'Father Abraham, have mercy on me, and send Lazarus to dip the end of his finger in water and cool my tongue, for I am in anguish in this flame.' But Abraham said, 'Child, remember that you in your lifetime received your good things, and Lazarus in like manner bad things; but now he is comforted here, and you are in anguish. And besides all this, between us and you a great chasm has been fixed, in order that those who would pass from here to you may not be able, and none may cross from there to us.'

This third story in the sequence also features a rich man. The other main character is a poor man, called Lazarus, who lay at his gate. Lazarus was neither the man's son, nor his manager. But, as the story unfolds, we learn that the rich man was aware of his existence and knew his name. Lazarus received nothing from the rich man. We are not told how Lazarus got into the sad state that he was in. He was hungry and hoped that he could at least get the crumbs that fell from the rich man's table – an attitude reminiscent of the prodigal son's desire for the pigswill. The rich man made no attempt to use his wealth to help Lazarus. The only comfort that he got was from the guard dogs (not pets, by the way – dogs were not kept as pets at that time) that showed him some sympathy by licking his sores.

Lazarus possessed nothing. He had no friends and so it would have been highly insensitive and cruel to have preached to him the lesson of the parable of the dishonest manager. How could you possibly tell a man like Lazarus to make friends with the mammon of unrighteousness (by being a gospel patron, for example), when he didn't have enough food or shelter and possessed nothing?

The two men die. Lazarus is honoured to be carried by the angels to Abraham's side in heaven. By contrast, the rich man finds himself in Hades, separated from God by an impassable gulf. Yet, perhaps to his amazement, the rich man can see Lazarus, in the far distance, in heaven, enjoying the company of no less than Abraham, one of the few people in Scripture to be called a friend of God (Jas. 2:23).

The main lesson is clear: God is a God of compensation. He can make up to people in the world to what they did not have in this life. He can supply a friend in that world, to the man who was friendless in this, through no fault of his own.

Luke also tells us about an encounter between Jesus and another very rich man, a ruler this time, very different in attitude from the rich man who had no time for Lazarus, or God.

THE RICH RULER (Luke 18:18-30)

> And a ruler asked him, 'Good Teacher, what must I do to inherit eternal life?' And Jesus said to him,' Why do you call me good? No one is good except God alone. You know the commandments: 'Do not commit adultery, Do not murder, Do not steal, Do not bear false witness, Honour your father and mother.' And he said, 'All these I have kept from my youth.' When Jesus heard this, he said to him, 'One thing you still lack. Sell all that you have and distribute to the poor, and you will have treasure in heaven; and come, follow me.' But when he heard these things, he became very sad, for he was extremely rich. Jesus, seeing that he had become sad, said, 'How difficult it is for those who have wealth to enter the kingdom of God! For it is easier for a camel to go through the eye of a needle than for a rich person to enter the kingdom of God.' Those who heard it said, 'Then who can be saved?' But he said, 'What is impossible with men is possible with God.' And Peter said, 'See, we have left our homes and followed you.' And he said to them, 'Truly, I say to you, there is no one who has left house or wife or brothers or parents or children, for the sake of the kingdom of God, who will not receive many times more in this time, and in the age to come eternal life.'

In a number of conversations with believers, who have considerable financial wealth, I have noticed a certain nervousness whenever the topic of giving is mentioned. Some have openly admitted that they fear that they may eventually be challenged to sell all that they possess, and give it to charity – a fear that inhibits their listening to any more on the topic (Luke 16:19-26).

In the opposite direction, other sincere believers have taken, what Jesus said to the Rich Ruler to apply directly to them and, without thinking it through adequately, they have sold all their possessions, and given the proceeds to charity. However, as a result, such people have sometimes become dependent on relatives (as I mentioned at the beginning of this book) which has resulted in the relatives being completely alienated from Christianity.

This is understandable since Christians are told that, if they do not provide for their dependents, they are worse than the heathen. Selling all you have, and giving it to the poor, is not consistent with that injunction. If you give away all your food, it is impossible to feed your family.

Furthermore, when Zacchaeus told the Lord that he was going to give half of his goods to the poor, Jesus did not reprimand him, and say that half was not enough, but that he must give all (Luke 19:1-10). Nor did Paul tell Lydia, when she was converted, to sell her home and give it to the poor. On the contrary, he was pleased to use that home as his base (Acts 16:11-15). There are many other similar examples. What they add up to is, at the very least, that the Lord expects believers to act as responsible stewards of their wealth.

What then shall we make of Jesus' encounter with this rich young ruler?

The context is that Jesus had been talking to the crowd about entering the kingdom of God, by receiving it as a child. The ruler, intrigued, asked Jesus what he had to do to inherit eternal life. His question shows that he thought that he could use his considerable wealth to pay for eternal life in the kingdom of God, just as he had been able to buy everything else up until then. The fact that he thought he could do so, also shows that he had not understood much about the King, or His kingdom. He addressed Jesus as 'Good teacher,' and must have been rocked back on his heels, by the reply: 'Why do you call me good? There is none good, but God.' Did he really mean to say that he thought Jesus was God? David Gooding comments:

> It was no theological quibble. If Jesus was in fact God incarnate, and the ruler had come to see that was so, then of course the ruler would be prepared to do whatever he said, without question. It would be nonsense to ask for admittance

into the kingdom, and yet from the very outset, to refuse to do what the king himself said. But the ruler was not prepared to do what Jesus told him. His "Good teacher" turned out to be mere polite talk.[4]

As for what he could do, did he not know God's commandments: five of which Jesus cited to him. Yes, he had kept those for years, he claimed. Gooding continues:

> He had come, we recall, asking what he had to do to inherit eternal life. Christ told him how he could have not only eternal life, but treasure in heaven (see [Luke] 18:22). But when he discovered that he would have to choose between treasure in heaven, and his considerable earthly possessions, he decided that the latter were, after all, the more valuable of the two. That is the difficulty with those who are, in any way, rich. Not only can preoccupation with possessions leave them unprepared for the judgments that will accompany the coming of the kingdom (see [Luke] 17:26-33), but their present possessions make the kingdom of God appear very much less than the one supremely valuable thing. It becomes at best a thing which they would gladly have in addition to their riches, if they could conveniently do so, but not something to be chosen, if need be, to the exclusion of all else. And as long as they think of the kingdom like that, it is doubtful if they will ever enter it.[5]

It seemed to the crowd around, that this made salvation impossible. Yet Jesus replied: 'What is impossible for men is possible with God.' And, indeed, there were men standing there, Jesus's disciples, who had taken the step of leaving all to follow Him. One of them, Peter, pointed this out, to which Jesus responded that every disciple who had left house, or relatives, for the sake of God's kingdom, would be abundantly compensated, not only in the world to come, but also in this life. In other words, Jesus promised to make up to them much more than they had left.

We don't know if the rich ruler heard this important principle that, if we put Jesus first as Lord and follow Him, then He will provide for us – but He has to be put first, which the ruler was not prepared to do. Later on, Paul could write

---

[4] *According to Luke*, p.311.

[5] Ibid, p.311.

that he suffered the loss of all things, yet his heart was full of gratitude for the ways in which the Lord had compensated him for that loss, for example, by giving him innumerable friends who cared for him.

Taking all of this into account, we see that the Lord does not deal with each individual in the same way, but according to his or her situation and needs. It is for us to respond, 'Yes Lord, I will do what you say,' and to leave the implications of that decision with Him. We need not fear that He will ever allow true response to His calling to contradict the principles and teaching He has laid down in Scripture.

THE PROBLEM OF CONTACT WITH EVIL

At this point we shall digress somewhat to think about the fact that there are many situations in life where it is very difficult, or impossible, to avoid contact with or dealing with evil in our work. We have already seen this in Jesus' teaching about what He called 'unrighteous' mammon, that is, money that was in some way tainted with unrighteousness in its journey through the economic system.

In order to understand different levels of engagement with evil, running through a spectrum from complete complicity to complete non-involvement, moral theologians and ethicists try to draw common sense distinctions between intentional and non-intentional cooperation, between active and passive cooperation, and between proximate (or physically close) cooperation and remote cooperation. They have also stressed the importance of looking for alternatives to the evil, and trying to balance levels of cooperation with evil against the morally good things that may result.[6]

The problem arises from the fact that we live in a fallen world. The entry of sin into the world through human disobedience to God, as described in Genesis 3, has damaged not only our relationship with God, but has damaged the whole of nature. The taint of sin is all-pervading. Our very engagement in complex and interconnected human society means that we sinful men and women find it difficult to avoid

---

[6]   See e.g. https://www.ewtn.com/vote/moral-cooperation-in-evil.asp

some degree of contact, cooperation, or even complicity, with evil.

Here are some more examples. Take the everyday matter of shopping for clothes and shoes. Tragically, some of what is on offer has been manufactured in factories using child labour. Once we learn, for example, that a certain internet giant is selling such items without concern about where they are sourced, then we have a choice. We don't have to go on buying there: we can make a moral decision to shop more ethically elsewhere.

What about the irresponsible use of plastics and other materials that are fouling up our oceans, and killing sea-life? The naturalist David Attenborough has made a number of magnificent films to shock people into taking this matter seriously.

What about eating chickens, and other livestock, that have been kept in unbelievably cruel conditions? Yet, we often eat them without a thought about how they have been treated?

What about the testing of cosmetics and medicines? Cosmetics used to be tested on animals without regard to their suffering – and yet many people used them without a thought as to where they came from. A 2019 article entitled *Bioethics: a look at animal testing in medicine and cosmetics in the UK,* by Stefane Kabene and Said Baadel, informs us that, thankfully, the use of animals for testing cosmetics products has been banned in the UK, and all other member states of the European Union since 2013. However, other countries like China, and the United States of America, still continue with the practice.

The authors also point out that about 50 to 100 million animals are used for experiments every year, and over 1.37 million animals were used for drug experimentation in America, in the year 2010. They say: 'Experimentation on human genetics presents various legal and ethical challenges to medical and biological researchers, alongside problems in creating experimental procedures using human test subjects. These problems occur partially due to the fact that the experimentation processes, involved in these types of studies, often lead to extensive gene, and physiological damages, to the test subjects. Such experiments typically involve deliberate presentation of diseases and other gene modifications to the test subjects, usually requiring the euthanizing of the involved subjects.'[7]

Have we even thought of checking whether the many medicines that we regularly use are ethically 'clean'? We need to be very careful before condemning a particular drug or vaccine because of its provenance, when we ourselves have been using drugs or vaccines, whose origins may be similar, but we know nothing about them.

In this and many other examples, knowledge makes a difference; a principle that arises in the New Testament, in connection with the question as to whether Christians should eat food that was sacrificed to idols, and then sold in the temple shambles.[8] Paul's ruling for the Corinthian church is that they, with a clear conscience before God, could and should eat food set before them, and should not themselves raise the issue of where the food had been sourced. However, if their hosts told them the food had been sacrificed to idols, then they should refuse, making clear their Christian view of idolatry.[9] Otherwise they would be complicit in the evils of idol worship. Knowledge makes a difference.

Another question that sometimes arises is whether we should leave employment where our employer is doing things that we would oppose as Christians, even if he does not require us to participate. As I see it, the answer here depends on what effect his behaviour has on the way in which I will be seen. For instance, suppose I am employed by a major food chain, whose CEO I do not even know personally, but he has a reputation for being unfaithful to his wife. As a believer, I do not approve of his behaviour, but it would be hard to imagine that my witness to my circle of contacts would be compromised by the fact that this man is the CEO of the company for which I work.

---

[7]   J Med Ethics Hist Med. 2019; 12: 15. Published online 2019 Nov 12. doi: 10.18502/jmehm.v12i15.1875

[8]   It should be noted that this is not the same issue as treated in Romans 14, where the food laws were originally God-given and had nothing to do with idol worship.

[9]   See 1 Corinthians 8.

Suppose on the other hand, however, that I am employed by a company whose board is discovered to be employing child labour abroad, paying less than subsistence money to foreign workers, and carrying out wholesale destruction of the environment. It is then quite possible that I would be seen to be complicit with such attitudes and would have to consider my position as a Christian.

I mentioned earlier the situation faced by some early Christian traders in cities like Corinth, who would normally have to belong to a trade guild in order for their business to prosper. Membership of such guilds often involved participating in ceremonies where food was eaten that had been sacrificed to pagan deities. Paul pointed out to such traders that they could not take the financial benefit without being spiritually involved, and therefore compromised.

To them Paul wrote:

> Do not be unequally yoked with unbelievers. For what partnership has righteousness with lawlessness? Or what fellowship has light with darkness? What accord has Christ with Belial? Or what portion does a believer share with an unbeliever? What agreement has the temple of God with idols? For we are the temple of the living God; as God said,
>
> I will make my dwelling among them and walk among them, and I will be their God, and they shall be my people. Therefore, go out from their midst, and be separate from them, says the Lord, and touch no unclean thing; then I will welcome you, and I will be a father to you, and you shall be sons and daughters to me, says the Lord Almighty. (2 Cor. 6:14-18)

It was a tough call, where God promised to be a father to those who were prepared to take the costly stand, and refuse to compromise by joining the guild, even though they would lose out.

However, we cannot always walk away, even if it is costly and difficult. We don't always have an opt out possibility. For instance, some of the money that we pay in taxes may well be used by the government for purposes that we think are wrong. Yet, Jesus Himself instructed people to pay taxes to Caesar (Mark 12:17) and, on the same principle, we today pay our taxes as a Christian duty. If we refused to do so, we might well be sent to prison, and that would involve us being complicit in having other taxpayers footing the bill for our unnecessary incarceration, scarcely a morally defensible position! Worse still, it would involve us putting our own family at risk, which is not permissible for a Christian. It is clear that the Lord does not regard us as complicit in any evil that the government may do with this tax revenue. No doubt He will hold them responsible. We must, therefore, leave the final judgement to Him.

Another evil is very widespread in certain parts of the world – the protection racket. For instance, the Mafia in Italy exert pressure on farmers to pay them, threatening that, if they fail to do so, their vineyards will be set on fire, their farm machinery stolen, or worse. What should Christians do? To refuse to pay might well mean loss of property, or loss of life. Some people faced with this kind of thing have told me that they feel they have to pay – regarding it as a kind of tax and settling it, because Jesus told us to pay our taxes.

Then there are many countries in the world where bribery is rife at every level of society, where nothing gets done unless a 'sweetener' is added to the contract. In such circumstances, Christians may find it difficult or impossible to run a business. Think of the situation where medicines are scarce, and believers cannot obtain them without a bribe. What should they do? Those taking the bribes might be impoverished and need the money themselves. Should we condemn such people, we who live in societies where, thankfully, such problems are rare? These issues are often heartbreakingly difficult, and there are no easy answers, so that we need to be very careful about taking the moral high ground and making premature judgements.

Also, the Apostle Paul told Christian believers in Rome: 'Let every person be subject to the governing authorities. For there is no authority except from God, and those that exist have been instituted by God' (Rom. 13:1). The emperor at the time was the brutal and unprincipled Nero. Paul, as a Roman citizen, also appealed to the Roman justice system, though he knew it was corrupt and very unlikely to be fair to his case: which it wasn't. It executed him.

Zacchaeus

Scripture itself engages with an aspect of this problem of contact with evil. Consider the famous incident described by Luke – a doctor, by the way – concerning Zacchaeus, a tax collector, hated by the locals because of his complicity with the Roman authorities that had made him very rich. He wanted to see Jesus as He passed by and, since he was short of stature, he climbed a tree to get a good view. Luke says: 'And when Jesus came to the place, he looked up and said to him, "Zacchaeus, hurry and come down, for I must stay at your house today." So, he hurried and came down and received him joyfully. And when they saw it, they all grumbled, "He has gone in to be the guest of a man who is a sinner"' (Luke 19:5-7).

Zacchaeus' house, and the food he served to the Lord Jesus as an honoured guest, were very likely to have been the products of his tax extortion, yet Jesus clearly accepted the hospitality. Jesus was sinless. He was not complicit in Zacchaeus' deeds, nor did He cooperate with, or in his evil, even though the onlookers thought that was precisely what He was doing – compromising Himself by accepting hospitality from a man who was a sinner.

In the event, Jesus' acceptance of Zacchaeus' invitation resulted in the man receiving Him joyfully. Zacchaeus then says to Jesus: 'And Zacchaeus stood and said to the Lord, "Behold, Lord, half of my goods I give to the poor. And if I have defrauded anyone of anything, I restore it fourfold." And Jesus said to him, "Today salvation has come to this house, since he also is a son of Abraham. For the Son of Man came to seek and to save the lost"' (Luke 19:8-10).

We are now about to see a brilliant illustration of the lesson that we have already drawn from the parable of the dishonest manager, about the use of 'unrighteous wealth'. Zacchaeus certainly had plenty of it when he met the Lord.

Then, Zacchaeus had a change of heart. He received salvation by faith in Jesus, so that Jesus could describe him as 'a true son of Abraham'. That experience transformed his attitude to his possessions. He realised that his wealth is seriously tainted by the extortion that produced it. Without any coercion on the part of Jesus, he said that he was going to give half of his goods to the poor; people from whom, presumably, Zacchaeus had not taken taxes, as they could not have afforded to pay them. It is important to see that Zacchaeus' salvation did not depend on his generosity. The generosity was the fruit of his salvation that proved it genuine. It was not the root of his salvation, for salvation is not of works (Eph. 2:8-9).

The result of Zacchaeus generosity was, of course, that the poor received and benefitted from stuff that had been obtained, as Zacchaeus admitted, by fraudulent means from taxpayers. But Jesus makes no statement to the effect that Zacchaeus should not do this, since it would make the recipients complicit in his evil deeds. Zacchaeus does not stop there. He pledges to restore fourfold the money that he had extorted from actual taxpayers. That meant that they also would benefit from his evil behaviour. But did it mean that they were tainted with evil? There is no hint of it.

The story of Zacchaeus can help us understand just how complex this matter is, but can also show us how to cope with it, and fulfil Paul's injunction not to be overcome by evil, but to overcome evil with good (Rom. 12:21). God can bring good out of evil.

These are only a few examples of the problems of living in a fallen world where evil lurks everywhere. We need to keep our moral and spiritual antennae finely tuned by Scripture and prayer, as we face difficult moral decisions before the Lord.

Strategic planning

Zacchaeus' repentance and conversation led at once to a desire to make reparations for what he had done, and Luke tells us about the strategy he adopted to carry out his intentions. However, many Christians have been entrusted with wealth that, unlike Zacchaeus, they have accumulated by honest means. They wish to distribute some of it but are faced with such a vast number of requests for help that they find it difficult to know where to begin. Also, many believers have shared with me their hurt and disappointment at the way in which they feel that their generosity has sometimes been abused, an experience that has left them bewildered and reluctant to get involved in supporting anything more. That reaction in turn leads to feelings of guilt, meanness, and stinginess. And this is not just the experience of very wealthy donors, as I sense that most, if not all, Christians have known such disappointments. There is, therefore, a need to address this issue without embarrassment, in order to come up with principles to help in future giving. I have consulted a number of people on this, and I'm grateful to them for sharing their wisdom with me, anonymously – understandably.

In addition, the Strategic Resource Group (SRG) – that links together what are called 'high-capacity givers' – have consulted their experienced donors to formulate principles of wise giving.

Firstly, before transferring money, especially substantial sums, take time and care to build trust and relationships with potential recipient individuals or organisations. This will involve getting to know the people running the projects in which you are interested, and asking straight questions about viability, transparency, cost-effectiveness, and sustainability, amongst other things. In other words, as responsible stewards of what the Lord has entrusted to us, we must do due diligence. That may involve getting to know other donors to the same projects and asking them about their experience. It may also involve finding out how much of the money given to the project goes on overheads and administration, and how much actually gets to the project itself. There is no virtue in irresponsibility. Beware of the 'just trust me' mentality.

Also beware of the 'money solves everything' mentality that is widespread in affluent societies. There is great danger in stressing the size of resources to deal with issues rather than first of all thinking through the nature of those issues. During the time of the Cold War when there was much interest in helping churches behind the Iron Curtain – a praiseworthy objective in itself. However, it became evident that some wealthy Western churches were exercising unhealthy control – even on the theology of certain groups – through their donations of money and literature. The risk of greed was great and I often heard humble believers in such countries complain of the destructive effect of Western money. Also, Christian organisations in the West were usually donor dependent so that in their literature they had to come up with 'thrilling' stories about what donor gifts had achieved. This gave rise to the temptation to exaggerate or even manufacture stories calculated to get people to reach deeper into their pockets.

Also beware of the 'money solves everything' mentality that is widespread in affluent societies. There is great danger in stressing the size of resources to deal with issues rather than first of all thinking through the nature of those issues. During the time of the Cold War when there was much interest in helping churches behind the iron curtain – a praiseworthy objective in itself. However, it became evident that some wealthy Western churches were exercising unhealthy control – even on the theology of certain groups - through their donations of money and literature. The risk of greed was great and I often heard humble believers in such countries complain of the destructive effect of Western money. Also, Christian organisations in the West were usually donor-dependent so that in their literature they had to come up with 'thrilling' stories about what donor gifts had achieved. This gave rise to the temptation to exaggerate or even manufacture stories calculated to get people to reach deeper into their pockets.

Questions

1. Where in your view did the Rich Fool go wrong? How can we avoid doing the same thing? To what extent should we prepare for the future?
2. Both the lost son and the dishonest manager wasted goods – what is the difference between them and what can we learn from it?
3. Does it matter if Christian believers waste their goods since they will, after all, be in heaven anyway?
4. What lesson does Jesus draw from the parable of the dishonest manager? How would you apply it to yourself? How can you make friends 'with the mammon of unrighteousness'?

5. Why do you think Jesus told the story of the Rich Man and Lazarus?
6. What is the main take-home message to be drawn from the story of the Rich Young Ruler?
7. Discuss the problem of unavoidable contact with evil, giving examples from your own experience.
8. Have you ever felt disappointed with what has happened to a gift you gave to Christian work?
9. What are the due-diligence steps that are important to you, before giving to a particular person, or cause? Discuss these issues with others.

CHAPTER 7

WORK'S ETERNAL REWARDS

**'Aim at heaven and you will get earth thrown in.
Aim at earth and you will get neither.'**

C. S. Lewis

In His teaching, the Lord Jesus constantly emphasised that there is a connection between what we do in this life, and our experience in the world to come. We can, He says, even increase the circle of our friends in eternity by our use of the by-products of our work here. This naturally leads us to what the Bible teaches on how we can use our wealth of various kinds, to maximize our effectiveness for the kingdom in partnership with others.

We have considered the purpose of work and the outcomes of work. We are now in a position to think about what Scripture has to say about the matter of (ultimate) reward for our work. This is a topic about which the first thing to say is that many Christians avoid it, because talk of reward, especially reward in heaven, can lead to accusations of being mercenary: 'If I do this, will you give me that?' Yet Jesus Himself did not shy away from teaching His disciples about reward, so it is not a matter that any follower of Jesus is at liberty to ignore. We should, rather, try to understand it, since Jesus' teaching from beginning to end reveals no hint of anything mercenary. Indeed, we would never think of ourselves as being mercenary because we receive a wage at the end of the month.

C.S. Lewis makes the following point:

> We must not be troubled by unbelievers when they say that this promise of reward makes the Christian life a mercenary affair. There are different kinds of reward. There is the reward which has no natural connection with the things you do to earn it, and is quite foreign to the desires that ought to accompany those things. Money is not the natural reward of love, that is why we call a man mercenary if he marries a woman for the sake of her money. But marriage is the proper reward for a real lover, and he is not mercenary for desiring it... The schoolboy beginning Greek grammar cannot look forward to his adult enjoyment of Sophocles as a lover looks forward to marriage or a general to victory. He has to begin by working for marks, or to escape punishment, or to please his parents, or, at best, in the hope of a future good which he cannot at present imagine or desire. His position, therefore, bears a certain resemblance to that of the mercenary; the reward he is going to get will, in actual fact, be a natural or proper reward, but he will not know that till he has got it...
>
> The Christian, in relation to heaven, is in much the same position as this schoolboy. Those who have attained everlasting life in the vision of God doubtless know very well that it is no mere bribe, but the very consummation of their earthly discipleship; but we who have not yet attained it cannot know this in the same way, and cannot even begin to know it at all except by continuing to obey and finding the first reward of our obedience in our increasing power to desire the ultimate reward.[1]

Lewis' insight helps us to understand what Scripture has to say about the way in which what we do with our (work) lives here on earth affects our lives in the world to come.

---

[1]   C.S. Lewis, *The Weight of Glory*, (New York, Macmillan, 1940), pp. 1–3.

However, before we think about that, we should remind ourselves of the lessons we have learned so far: that entrance to the presence of God in heaven is *not* a reward. We cannot earn our place in heaven, as many people misguidedly think. Salvation is by grace, through faith and not by meritorious works. Paul writes:

> Now to the one who works, his wages are not counted as a gift but as his due. And to the one who does not work but believes in him who justifies the ungodly, his faith is counted as righteousness, just as David also speaks of the blessing of the one to whom God counts righteousness apart from works: 'Blessed are those whose lawless deeds are forgiven, and whose sins are covered; blessed is the man against whom the Lord will not count his sin.' (Rom. 4:4-9)

This could scarcely be expressed more clearly: 'To the one who does *not* work...' Nor is it the case that faith is needed to do the works that earn salvation, as some people imagine. No. Faith in Christ is the very opposite of work. Salvation involves being born again, that is, receiving eternal life, about which Jesus says: 'Truly, truly, I say to you, whoever hears my word and believes him who sent me has eternal life. He does not come into judgement but has passed from death to life' (John 5:24).

In John 5, Jesus has been speaking of Himself as the God-appointed final Judge of mankind. As the Judge, He categorically states that those who believe in Him will 'not come into judgement'. This is implied in the words of David cited from Romans 4 above. The believer in Christ will never face the penalty of their sins at that Great White Throne of final judgement as Christ has paid that penalty for them. This is the magnificent gospel.

This does not mean that believers will never face assessment for what they have done with their lives in general and in their work in particular. That is a very different matter. Scripture teaches that there will be such an assessment at what is called the 'judgement seat'. Paul explains what is involved: 'So whether we are at home or away, we make it our aim to please him. For we must all appear before the judgement seat of Christ, so that each one may receive what is due for what he has done in the body, whether good or evil. Therefore, knowing the fear of the Lord, we persuade others. But what we are is known to God, and I hope it is known also to your conscience' (2 Cor. 5:6-11).

Paul is writing to believers, not to the world in general, about what happens at death. While still on earth, Paul makes it his aim to please the Lord. The reason he gives for that here, is that: 'we must all appear before the judgement seat of Christ, so that each one may receive what is due for what he has done in the body, whether good or evil' (2 Cor. 5:10).

The issue at the judgement seat of Christ is assessment and recompense for what believers have done in their lives. It cannot be, and indeed is not, salvation, which is not of works. The matter to be dealt with at Christ's judgement seat is reward for works – not salvation. Paul further explains how the judgement seat of Christ will operate: 'Why do you pass judgement on your brother? Or you, why do you despise your brother? For we will all stand before the judgement seat of God; for it is written, "As I live, says the Lord, every knee shall bow to me, and every tongue shall confess to God." So, then each of us will give an account of himself to God' (Rom. 14:10-12).

Paul warns the believers in Rome to be careful with their assessment of others, since, one day, they will have to account for themselves to God. This would appear to imply that this judgement will not simply be the reading out of a verdict, accompanied by appropriate reward, but will involve the person being judged giving an account of themselves. We get an additional insight into this process in our Lord's teaching in His Sermon on the Mount:

> Judge not, that you be not judged. For with the judgement you pronounce you will be judged, and with the measure you use it will be measured to you. Why do you see the speck that is in your brother's eye, but do not notice the log that is in your own eye? Or how can you say to your brother, 'Let me take the speck out of your eye,' when there is the log in your own eye? You hypocrite, first take the log out of your own eye, and then you will see clearly to take the speck out of your brother's eye. (Matt. 7:1-5)

Could the principle enunciated in verse 2 be reasonably imagined as follows? Think of all the judgements that we have made of others, especially those we work with, in the last month, say. Now imagine that these judgements are analysed to find the criteria that we used to make them. Finally, imagine that these criteria, our criteria, are used by the Lord to assess our own behaviour and work. That prospect would not exactly fill many of us with joyful expectation, would it? Yet, we certainly could not argue that it was inappropriate or unfair. And that is exactly what is going to happen.

Paul and the Lord are using anticipation of the judgement seat of Christ to encourage people to control their attitudes to others and their behaviour here on earth. It accords with the old adage: 'best sort it out now than wait until the Lord has to sort it out for us'. We need to take this seriously in all aspects of our lives, particularly in our families and in our workplaces. An added reason for so doing is seen from the further insight that Paul gives us into this final assessment of our lives:

> According to the grace of God given to me, like a skilled master builder I laid a foundation, and someone else is building upon it. Let each one take care how he builds upon it. For no one can lay a foundation other than that which is laid, which is Jesus Christ. Now if anyone builds on the foundation with gold, silver, precious stones, wood, hay, straw – each one's work will become manifest, for the Day will disclose it, because it will be revealed by fire, and the fire will test what sort of work each one has done. If the work that anyone has built on the foundation survives, he will receive a reward. If anyone's work is burned up, he will suffer loss, though he himself will be saved, but only as through fire. (1 Cor. 3:10-15)

Here, Paul likens our lives as believers as buildings in progress, and he distinguishes carefully between their foundations and superstructure. The foundation of a believer's life is Christ, and Christ alone. But what we build on, that foundation will vary in quality for each of us, and that quality matters, since, one day, it will be tested by fire. Not, incidentally, the fire of purgatory. When Jesus is pictured as judge in Revelation 1, He is seen to have *'eyes* as a flame of fire'. The judgement consists in scrutiny by those eyes. Paul is not telling us this to scare us. We should remember that the Judge, with those all-seeing eyes, is the one who 'loved us and loosed us from our sins in his blood'. Paul is informing us of this so that our awareness of what will happen in the future influences how we live in the present. C.S. Lewis puts it beautifully: 'Not hoping to get to heaven as a reward for your actions, but inevitably wanting to act in a certain way because a first faint gleam of heaven is already inside you.'[2]

We need to face the fact that if we build unacceptable rubbish into our lives as Christians, one day it will all be burnt away, and we shall suffer loss. However, Paul is careful to say that the loss that will be incurred is not the loss of salvation. He adds that the persons themselves will be saved, but as by fire. He still insists that salvation itself does not depend on works, and so is not forfeitable. We deduce from this the following:

Principle: Believers will one day after death be assessed by the Lord, not to determine whether they are saved or not, but to assess the quality of what they have done during their lives, and to be recompensed for it, either positively or negatively.

Taking this principle seriously would make a huge difference in every part of our lives, the workplace in particular. Just think of all the gossip, backstabbing, character assassination, false description of goods or accounts, inflation of qualifications, inaccurate reporting – an endless list of things that go on in offices, workshops, hospitals, board-rooms, etc., etc. What a difference it would make if, before we assess someone else, we stopped to think that the criteria upon which we make that judgement might well be used one day to assess us.

---

[2] *Mere Christianity* (London: Harper Collins) Book III, Chapter 12.

Reward for following the Lord

In order to get the full picture, we now look at what Jesus taught specifically to His disciples about reward on one occasion when Peter asked Him about the topic. Then Peter said in reply, 'See, we have left everything and followed you. What then will we have?' Jesus said to them, 'Truly, I say to you, in the new world, when the Son of Man will sit on his glorious throne, you who have followed me will also sit on twelve thrones, judging the twelve tribes of Israel. And everyone who has left houses or brothers or sisters or father or mother or children or lands, for my name's sake, will receive a hundredfold and will inherit eternal life. But many who are first will be last, and the last first' (Matthew 19:27-30).

Jesus did not rebuke Peter for his question, nor accuse him of having a mercenary attitude. Jesus gave him a clear answer. A day would come when Jesus, the Son of Man would sit on His glorious throne. Later in Matthew Jesus says that this would happen 'in the resurrection'. At that time, the apostles would have a special role and sit on twelve thrones judging the twelve tribes of Israel. As for others, Jesus says, there will be a hundredfold (ten thousand percent!) recompense for what believers have had to leave for Christ's sake. The interest offered by the bank of heaven is off the scale, compared with the best rates ever by a bank on earth. Notice what is included – not only material possessions such as houses and land, but people. Perhaps a hint here about the making of friends discussed in the parable of the dishonest steward?

Jesus then makes a rather enigmatic statement: *'But many who are first will be last, and the last first.'* Presumably, this is not said to negate what has gone before, but rather as a principle that operates above and beyond what has just been enunciated. It is clearly important, since Jesus devotes an entire parable to explain it – the famous parable of the workers in the vineyard:

> For the kingdom of heaven is like a master of a house who went out early in the morning to hire labourers for his vineyard. After agreeing with the labourers for a denarius a day, he sent them into his vineyard. And going out about the third hour he saw others standing idle in the marketplace, and to them he said, "You go into the vineyard too, and whatever

is right I will give you." So they went. Going out again about the sixth hour and the ninth hour, he did the same. And about the eleventh hour he went out and found others standing. And he said to them, "Why do you stand here idle all day?" They said to him, "Because no one has hired us." He said to them, "You go into the vineyard too." And when evening came, the owner of the vineyard said to his foreman, "Call the labourers and pay them their wages, beginning with the last, up to the first." And when those hired about the eleventh hour came, each of them received a denarius. Now when those hired first came, they thought they would receive more, but each of them also received a denarius. And on receiving it they grumbled at the master of the house, saying, "These last worked only one hour, and you have made them equal to us who have borne the burden of the day and the scorching heat." But he replied to one of them, "Friend, I am doing you no wrong. Did you not agree with me for a denarius? Take what belongs to you and go. I choose to give to this last worker as I give to you. Am I not allowed to do what I choose with what belongs to me? Or do you begrudge my generosity?" So the last will be first, and the first last. (Matt. 20:1-16)

The vineyard owner, unusually for that day and age, goes personally to the marketplace to hire workers for his vineyard, and, even more unusually, makes five separate trips in one day. He agrees a wage with the first group, but to the other four groups he says that he will give whatever is right. At the end of the day the vineyard owner gets his foreman to line up the workers in their groups beginning with the last and ending with the first. The foreman pays them all the same, a denarius each, the going rate for a day's work.

Those that had worked the entire day grumbled when they saw the distribution of pay. Why had they only received one denarius when they had worked for many more hours than those who came later? The owner responded: 'Friend, I am doing you no wrong. Did you not agree with me for a denarius? Take what belongs to you and go. I choose to give to this last worker as I give to you. Am I not allowed to do what I choose with what belongs to me? Or do you begrudge my generosity?'

The man had, in fact, no right to complain because he had *agreed* to the wage in advance. The others had trusted the owner to pay them what was right. And the owner had every right to be generous, the money was his, he was free to do what he liked with it.

There is an important principle here. There is a danger lurking when we ask the Lord, Peter's question about what reward we shall receive. The danger is that we run the risk of losing out by being mercenary and trying to make a bargain with the Lord. The parable teaches that striking a bargain with God is not a wise thing to do. For, we may well end up being last rather than first. What is more, we shall have no reason to complain. God is likely to be far more generous than we can imagine, so we can safely leave the matter of reward to Him.

Most of us are familiar with the idea of reward for work done. However, there is another aspect of reward with which we may well be less familiar – that is, reward for character developed during life. The main principle here is to be found in the teaching of the apostle Peter.

Principle: The quality of our entrance to the future kingdom is linked to the character we have developed in this life.

The relevant passage is 2 Peter 1:10-11: 'Therefore, brothers, be all the more diligent to confirm your calling and election, for if you practise these qualities, you will never fall. For in this way there will be richly provided for you an entrance into the eternal kingdom of our Lord and Saviour Jesus Christ.'[3]

Peter is writing: 'To those who have obtained a faith of equal standing with ours by the righteousness of our God and Saviour Jesus Christ' (2 Pet. 1:1). That is, his audience is one of believers who, because salvation is by faith and not works, possess a faith of equal standing with that of an apostle. In Paul's language, they all are standing on the one and only true foundation, Jesus Christ. The thrust of the passage is that they should build on that foundation. God has the resource to enable them, through getting to know Him better, to develop Christian character traits: faith, hope, and love, and the virtues of knowledge, self-control, steadfastness, godliness, brotherly

---

[3] In order to see this passage in context, you are encouraged to read 2 Peter 1:3-11.

affection, together with the four cardinal virtues of prudence, justice, fortitude, and temperance, and other classic virtues like courage and fidelity.

Why should they, and we, bother? Firstly, because co-operating with the Lord in growing these qualities of excellence increases both our effectiveness and our fruitfulness. The person who lacks them is being short-sighted and inconsistent, having forgotten what salvation is about – dealing with sin.

All believers are therefore called upon to *confirm* their 'calling and election'. That does not mean that they are uncertain and need to get assurance, though that may be an additional problem for some. It means that they are to confirm that their salvation is real, by the moral and spiritual quality of their lives. As the apostle James would put it, they are to demonstrate that their faith in Christ is genuine by the goodness of their character and works.

Not only that, and this is the central principle; it makes an eternal difference whether we cooperate with the Lord in developing our Christian character, or not. The main point of Peter's argument is in verse 11: 'For in this way there will be richly provided for you an entrance into the eternal kingdom of our Lord and Saviour Jesus Christ.'

In the original Greek text, the word *'richly'* comes first in the word order, indicating that it is the keyword in the sentence. Peter is not contradicting what he said in verse 1 by making entrance into the kingdom conditional on Christian growth. Entrance to that kingdom is gained by responding to the grace of God in Jesus Christ and, like Nicodemus, being born again. Also, Peter is not speaking here about heavenly reward for work done, but rather, richness of entrance into the eternal kingdom for developed character.

Therefore, Peter is not discussing the difference between getting into the kingdom, or not getting in. He is speaking of something entirely different: the *richness or quality* of entrance into that kingdom. He tells us that it depends on whether or not we grow in these qualities as believers. What does he mean by this statement that may well initially strike us as puzzling?

We can dismiss the idea that it means that some believers will get to the centre of heaven where Jesus is, and others will have to be content to be on the periphery – if those terms even make sense. For, being in the immediate presence of the Lord is the birthright of all believers.

The clue as to what Peter means, lies in his double emphasis on the knowledge of God, and the knowledge of the Lord Jesus Christ. Consider an illustration. It is James' fourth birthday, and he is having a wonderful time, sitting on the sofa, knocking balloons around with his dad. As he sees it, his dad is the best dad in all the world, who fills his birthday with joy. James has no sense of missing anything, as his dad satisfies all his needs. The years pass, and James is now doing research at university in aerospace engineering, having been taught for a while by his dad, who is a physicist. Once again it is James' birthday. He and his dad are once again sitting on the sofa, but they are not knocking balloons around. They are having an animated conversation on the latest ideas in engineering physics. James, because he has conversed with him over the years, has a much deeper entrance into his dad than he did when he was four. But he could not have had the present conversation, if he had shown no real interest in what his dad thought or did.

It makes sense, surely, to think that this is the kind of thinking that lies behind what Peter says: that, if we draw on the Lord's proffered resources and, through His power, get to know Him better and better, we shall be able to enter much more deeply into His fellowship, than if we don't really bother to cultivate that fellowship.

Principle: We affect the quality or richness of our entry into the eternal kingdom of the Lord Jesus Christ by the extent of our character development, and increase in getting to know Him.

Peter is far from finished at this point. He goes on to tell how he shall soon make his exit (literally, *exodus*) from this world, and go out into that other world. In light of that, he wishes his readers to grasp as maximally important that the other world, the eternal world, in which he is encouraging them to invest their lives, is real. Peter's experience of the transfiguration convinced him that the power and the coming of the Lord Jesus were no cunningly devised myth. He, along with James and John, had seen the Lord in glory, and heard the very voice of God from heaven. They had directly experienced the extraordinary supernatural power of God in introducing them to Moses and Elijah in the company of Jesus. They believed the eternal world was real for the simple reason that they had been there and experienced it.

Heaven: Retirement from Work?

In everyday life, we are familiar with the idea that sooner or later we shall no longer have the energy to work as we once did, and many hope that one by-product of their work, their earnings, will help them finance their retirement. This has given rise to the idea that heaven is a kind of retirement community with little activity beyond the endless singing of hymns. Now there is nothing wrong with hymn-singing and most of us enjoy it, at least in moderate doses. But the idea of an eternal rest home with endless singing can be seriously off-putting.

In any case, the truth is very different. Earlier, we cited C.S. Lewis to the effect that rewards are of different kinds. There are proper rewards, like marriage being the proper reward of love, and there are mercenary rewards, like marrying for money. When it comes to the proper heavenly reward for work, we find that at least one aspect of it is the opposite of retirement: it is the opportunity to do more work. Jesus used His parable of the talents to teach us this – read Luke 19:11-27 at this point.

Jesus told this parable on His journey to Jerusalem as a reply to people who thought that He was about to inaugurate the visible kingdom of God. This was not to be the case, as He was about to explain. Jesus, like the nobleman in the parable, was going to go away for a time (to heaven) in order to be granted the authority to rule, and then He would return.

The storyline is that the nobleman, before he departed, entrusted each of three of his servants with a mina each, which, according to some scholars, is roughly equivalent to four month's wages for an average worker at the time. He encouraged them to use this money to engage in business until he returned. After he left, there was a rebellion among the citizens against him, and they sent a delegation after him saying they did not want him as their king.

Nevertheless, in spite of this hostility, he did return, and summoned the workers to see how they had fared in business in such adverse circumstances. Two of the servants had made a profit: the first, a thousand percent and the second five hundred. The nobleman, now king, rewarded them by giving them administrative responsibility over ten and five cities, respectively. That is, the reward for working was the opportunity to do more work, albeit of a different kind.

The parable clearly teaches us a number of things about the Lord's return. Firstly, that when he returns, he will reign, and his servants will reign with him. Peter had already learned this from Jesus: 'You shall sit on twelve thrones.' Paul says essentially the same: 'The saying is trustworthy, for: If we have died with him, we will also live with him; if we endure, we will also reign with him; if we deny him, he also will deny us: if we are faithless, he remains faithful – for he cannot deny himself' (2 Tim. 2:11-13).

Similarly, John writes: 'The one who conquers, I will grant him to sit with me on my throne, as I also conquered and sat down with my Father on his throne' (Rev. 3:21).

The notion of Christ's servants being actively involved in reigning – at a very high level, it would appear – is indicated in several other places:

> When one of you has a grievance against another, does he dare go to law before the unrighteous instead of the saints? Or do you not know that the saints will judge the world? And if the world is to be judged by you, are you incompetent to try trivial cases? Do you not know that we are to judge angels? How much more, then, matters pertaining to this life!' (1 Cor. 6:1-3)

From all of this it is abundantly clear that heaven will be no boring rest home, but a hive of fascinating activity where the skills and experience developed on earth will be transformed into something higher, richer, and infinitely satisfying. It goes way beyond all that we can ask or think. It is also apparent from the parable of the minas, that the amount of responsibility that any of us will have in that day will depend on our faithfulness in this life.

We should not forget, however, that there was a third servant in the parable who did not even try to engage in business with the money that had been entrusted to him. When eventually called to account the king removed his mina, and gave it to the servant who had made the most profit. The question arises as to how we are to understand this? Is it possible that this servant represents a believer? After all, in a similar sounding parable of the talents, recorded in Matthew 25:24-30, the servant who does not employ his talent is thrown into outer darkness. However, the parable of the minas in Luke is different. The man who did not invest his mina is not said to be thrown out. Indeed, the text clearly separates him from the enemies of the king, who do suffer his wrath: 'But as for these my enemies ...'

David Gooding makes the following helpful observation:

> What is it then, that still makes it difficult to think that the unfaithful servant in our parable represents a true believer? It is his whole concept of the King. Asked to account for his failure to work for his lord, he replies that it is his lord's failure for being a person who always expected to get something for nothing, to get something out where he put nothing in (Luke 19:21). Fear of him, fear of doing wrong, he says, has paralysed him.

> Our question, then, resolves itself into this: could anyone who truly believes that Christ gave his life for him, ever turn around and tell the Lord that in asking him to work for him, the Lord was asking something for nothing? People can be ungrateful, witness the nine lepers. But would a believer ever be so ungrateful? And would anyone who believes that Christ's death has secured him forgiveness for all of his sins, ever tell Christ that he was afraid to work for him in case he made a mistake?

> Perhaps our question is too theoretical, or too literary. Perhaps we had better ask ourselves what we imagine our own behaviour is even now telling the Lord about ourselves and what we think

of him, if we likewise are not faithfully engaged on the business he has entrusted to our care.

Believer or unbeliever, the unfaithful servant had his pound taken away. Failure to work for the Lord will not cost a believer his salvation: but it will certainly cost him his reward.

Let us end, however, on a happier note. The leper who was grateful to the Lord for what he had done for him and returned to give him thanks, found that his gratitude led on to something higher: in addition to his healing, he received the gift of salvation. So, the servant in our parable who worked faithfully for the Lord found his faithfulness had a snowball effect. The one pound gained ten; the ten pounds gained him authority over ten cities; and over and above all that he was given the unfaithful servant's pound as well. Given his way with pounds, this additional pound would soon turn itself into an additional city. It is a law of the kingdom, apparently, that to the one who already has, more shall be given.[4]

The fact that our work not only has a temporal but also an eternal significance is one of the unique glories of the Christian faith. It is also an answer to those who think that the gospel message is crude and cheap, in that it offers us a free ticket to heaven so that it doesn't matter how we subsequently behave.

It should also be a source of great wonder and encouragement to us that God is interested in our work. Furthermore, if we work as unto the Lord, then we are effectively investing in the world to come. Far from physical death bringing an end to all that we have done, it will be the doorway into a vastly greater experience of God in a world where there will be work for all, a world where, as the apostle John says: 'his servants shall serve him' (Rev. 22:3, KJV).

The guarantee of all of this is the fact that God has raised His Son from the dead. As we come to the end of this chapter we can say with Paul: '... thanks be to God, who gives us the victory through our Lord Jesus Christ. Therefore, my beloved brothers, be steadfast, immovable, always abounding in the work of the Lord, knowing that in the Lord your labour is not in vain' (1 Cor. 15:57-58).

---

[4]   D W Gooding, *According to Luke*, (Belfast: Myrtlefield House, 2013), 317-318.

I once saw in someone's office a large, printed notice citing the last nine words above. Perhaps it would be a good idea to do the same in our workplaces, whether at home, office, school, shop, farm, hospital, pulpit, etc., etc. We need reminding of its truth every day:

'In the Lord your labour is not in vain'.

From time to time I wonder whether, when in a day to come the glory of heaven dawns on me, my instinctive reaction will be: 'If I had realised it was going to be like this, I would have invested much more in it.'

William Tyndale's last words as he was engulfed in flames were: 'Lord, open the King of England's eyes.' We might do well to pray the same for ourselves: 'Lord open our eyes to see the reality of eternity and what we can do to invest in Your kingdom.'

Questions

1. Discuss the embarrassment some people feel when the topic of reward comes up. How can you deal with that embarrassment?
2. Is reward bribery? Does your answer depend on the context? Give reasons for your answer.
3. What do you say to those who jeer at you and say that your concept of salvation is 'pie in the sky when we die'?
4. Is salvation itself a reward? Give reasons for your example.
5. What is the judgement seat of Christ? What will happen there and how will it affect you? Does it matter?
6. What rewards did Jesus promise His disciples? What is meant by 'the first shall be last and the last shall be first'?
7. How does the development of Christian character affect our eternity? What should encourage us to take this seriously?
8. What does entrance into the kingdom involve?
9. How do you respond to those who suggest heaven is a retirement home?
10. What effect does the hope of Christ's return have on your life?

APPENDIX A

PRINCIPLES OF GOSPEL SUPPORT

The New Testament has quite a bit to say about the way in which gospel outreach should be supported. We shall find that it is highly instructive even though sometimes rather complex.

First, here is an important statement of key principles that Paul wrote to the Corinthian church:

> 'Am I not free? Am I not an apostle? Have I not seen Jesus our Lord? Are not you my workmanship in the Lord? If to others I am not an apostle, at least I am to you, for you are the seal of my apostleship in the Lord.
>
> This is my defence to those who would examine me. Do we not have the right to eat and drink? Do we not have the right to take along a believing wife, as do the other apostles and the brothers of the Lord and Cephas? Or is it only Barnabas and I who have no right to refrain from working for a living? Who serves as a soldier at his own expense? Who plants a vineyard without eating any of its fruit? Or who tends a flock without getting some of the milk?
>
> Do I say these things on human authority? Does not the Law say the same? For it is written in the Law of Moses, 'You shall not muzzle an ox when it treads out the grain.' Is it for oxen that

> God is concerned? Does he not certainly speak for our sake? It
> was written for our sake, because the ploughman should plough
> in hope and the thresher thresh in hope of sharing in the crop.
> If we have sown spiritual things among you, is it too much if
> we reap material things from you? If others share this rightful
> claim on you, do not we even more? (1 Cor. 9:1-12)

We must never forget that Paul was an apostle in a unique
position, and so we must be careful when applying what he
says about himself, and his ministry, to ourselves and our
ministries. As an evangelist, Paul had the right in common
with other evangelists to be supported by the Christian
community. He names some who take advantage of those
rights. However, he himself, though he could legitimately do
the same, chooses not to in the interests of the gospel. The
passage is very illuminating, and as we read it we should bear
in mind that there were those in the church at Corinth who
were very critical, indeed, suspicious of Paul and his motives
– even to the extent of questioning his apostleship.

Paul speaks of the basic right of an evangelist to eat and
drink, and to have that food supplied by the Christian
community; no one would surely deny him that. Furthermore,
there was a right for an evangelist to 'take along a believing
wife'.

Paul's use of the adjective 'believing' underlines the
importance for married evangelists of having a spouse that
shares their faith, particularly in the context of the kind
of ministry and work in which the early Christians were
engaged. Travel was dangerous, there were all kinds of perils
as Paul points out elsewhere, and, for the married, support of
the spouse was critically important.

Paul is, however, saying more than that. The expression
'take along a believing wife', which may seem odd to us, does
not simply mean 'to be married'; it means the right to take a
wife along with you, in your travels, in the Lord's service. The
other apostles did this, as did Jesus' brothers and Cephas, or
Peter, as well. Paul asserts Peter's right to expect the churches
he served on his travels to cover, not only his, but his wife's,
living expenses. In the past, perhaps, more than the present,
the denial of that right by churches and organisations, often

simply in order to save money, has put unnecessary strain on many marriages. It is ironic that a church, or organisation, that prides itself on standing for family values, can thoughtlessly create marital strain in the lives of those it has invited to do work, by failing to practise those values itself.

In order to support his case, Paul cites three examples from local life: the army, viticulture, and animal husbandry. Soldiers are paid for their work, they do not do it for free; vineyard owners have a clear right to live from their produce, as do those who tend sheep. To emphasise the importance of the underlying principle, Paul backs it up from Scripture: 'For it is written in the Law of Moses, "You shall not muzzle an ox when it treads out the grain." Is it for oxen that God is concerned? Does he not certainly speak for our sake?' (1 Cor. 9:9-10).

Paul's application is: 'If we have sown spiritual things among you, is it too much if we reap material things from you? If others share this rightful claim on you, do not we even more?' (1 Cor. 9:11). It is fundamental for Paul that spiritual help should neither be taken for granted, nor go unrecompensed: 'Let the one who is taught the word share all good things with the one who teaches' (Gal. 6:6).

This principle is not only applicable to evangelists and teachers but to all believers. It may be negatively illustrated by the following actual case. There was a busy lawyer who, though a believer, as sometimes happens with such people in all walks of life, had not developed his understanding of spiritual things much beyond a very elementary level, by contrast with his professional capacities. His daughter went to university and came back full of doubts and questions. She asked her father for help, but he couldn't understand her questions, let alone answer them. Eventually he enlisted the help of a woman he knew in the church who, although of humble standing, had spent time learning how to deal with the difficult questions that young people asked about their Christian faith, and was known to have helped many. After a time, she was able to resolve the daughter's issues and help restore her confidence in the Lord.

Sometime later, the woman was herself faced with a legal problem regarding the little business that she was trying to keep going, hand to mouth, since the death of her husband. She turned to the lawyer for help, and he easily sorted out the situation – and then billed her full whack for doing so. She had freely shared her knowledge of spiritual things, but he had not reciprocated by blessing her with his material things. Why not? Because his sense of values was not informed by Scripture. He had not understood the implications of Paul's teaching: 'Let the one who is taught the word share all good things with the one who teaches' (Gal. 6:6).

Paul, however, did not always use that right. He goes on to say:

> Nevertheless, we have not made use of this right, but we endure anything rather than put an obstacle in the way of the gospel of Christ. Do you not know that those who are employed in the temple service get their food from the temple, and those who serve at the altar share in the sacrificial offerings? In the same way, the Lord commanded that those who proclaim the gospel should get their living by the gospel. But I have made no use of any of these rights, nor am I writing these things to secure any such provision. For I would rather die than have anyone deprive me of my ground for boasting. For if I preach the gospel, that gives me no ground for boasting. For necessity is laid upon me. Woe to me if I do not preach the gospel! For if I do this of my own will, I have a reward, but if not of my own will, I am still entrusted with a stewardship. What then is my reward? That in my preaching I may present the gospel free of charge, so as not to make full use of my right in the gospel. (1 Cor. 9:12-18)

Paul's motivation in sometimes not using his right to support was to avoid any potential obstacle for the gospel. For instance, as he explains to the Corinthians, he took special pride in preaching the gospel in their wealthy city without looking to it for support. Paul, like every Jewish Rabbi, had a trade that supported his needs, and gave him credibility. If he was going to teach people who were for the most part employed, he needed to be seen to know what that was like. His trade was tent-making, a highly skilled and creative activity, much sought after in the ancient world. He did not abandon this trade when he became a Christian. He made use of it in order to finance, not only himself, but his team, as they went about their missionary work. After all, his pioneer work in hitherto unreached places preceded, by definition, the existence of churches that could have supported him. Paul made tents and ordered the various strands of his life – reinforcing what we learned from Genesis 1.

Referring to Paul's practical skill, the concept of 'tent making' has, rather sadly, come to mean for many people the equivalent of: 'I am not really interested in the work or business I do, but I do it in order to finance myself while I get on with my Christian work'. That can have the effect of severely devaluing work. Paul's tent-making was part of his Christian work. It was also highly skilled. He did it for the Lord.

Beyond the earnings from his trade, there were occasions when Paul did accept the support of others with gratitude. For instance, he writes to the church at Philippi, that he himself had founded:

> I rejoiced in the Lord greatly that now at length you have revived your concern for me. You were indeed concerned for me, but you had no opportunity. Not that I am speaking of being in need, for I have learned in whatever situation I am to be content. I know how to be brought low, and I know how to abound. In any and every circumstance, I have learned the secret of facing plenty and hunger, abundance and need. I can do all things through him who strengthens me.

> Yet it was kind of you to share my trouble. And you Philippians yourselves know that in the beginning of the gospel, when I left Macedonia, no church entered into partnership with me in giving and receiving, except you only. Even in Thessalonica you sent me help for my needs once and again. Not that I seek the gift, but I seek the fruit that increases to your credit I have received full payment, and more. I am well supplied, having received from Epaphroditus the gifts you sent, a fragrant offering, a sacrifice acceptable and pleasing to God. And my God will supply every need of yours according to his riches in glory in Christ Jesus. To our God and Father be glory forever and ever. Amen. (Phil. 4:10-20)

This is a very sensitively written letter that shows Paul's keen awareness of the pitfalls surrounding financial support, especially the dangers for recipients. The occasion was that Paul had just received some material help from the Philippian church, which, by contrast with the church at Corinth, was far from wealthy. He expresses his appreciation and gratitude for their long-standing concern that they had had no opportunity until then, to put it into action.

However, Paul does not wish his gratitude to be taken as a subtle hint that he is in need, and would like them to send him even more. Far from it, he has learned something that is very difficult for most of us: to rise above his circumstances, and be content with whatever state he finds himself in, whether it is one of abundance or deprivation. This he achieves, not in his own strength, but through that which God supplies to him.

Having cleared up that point, he returns to expressing his gratitude for the fact that the Philippians had supported him from the very beginning and were, for a while, the only church to do so. He regards what they did as a partnership between them and him, giving and receiving. He reminds them once more that he is not seeking their gift, but was looking out for the fruit of their conversion, represented by that gift. He finishes by saying that he had received the gift from Epaphroditus, and recognizes that it constituted a sacrifice for them. He reassures them that God would in turn fulfil their needs.

A simple observation that is so obvious we can easily miss it, is that Paul wrote letters about his support and that of others. He was meticulous about acknowledging the contributions that others made to his welfare, and that of other Christians and the churches in general. He never forgot to say thank you in writing. Nor should we.

I am of course aware that the organisational structure of some churches and Christian organisations is quite complicated so that, for an example, a salaried pastor might have a travelling or missionary remit that is funded by their home church/organisation, so that they can, say, go and preach and teach in a country where the Christians simply could not afford to pay their fare, or accommodation. In such cases it is important that the recipients should be given explicit names and addresses of those who made it possible for the visit, and encouraged to write and thank them. For instance, when I travelled in earlier days to Iron Curtain countries, it was a thrill, for those who helped with my travel, to receive a letter from people over there, expressing their thanks.

We now return to the passage cited above, from Philippians 4 – to pick up another important principle. Paul speaks about contentment; he knows how to take the ups and the downs of life in his stride. Similarly, Luke tells us about a group of soldiers who come to John the Baptist, asking what they should do. He replied: 'Do not extort money from anyone by threats or by false accusation and be content with your wages' (Luke 3:14). This does not necessarily mean that they were to be satisfied with what they were earning, and should not attempt to improve their situation. Indeed, John's warning about extortion indicates that they were underpaid. The danger is that, in order to improve an unfair situation, we may be tempted to resort to making threats or false accusations. However, in some employment situations today, there are mechanisms of appeal, line managers, supervisors, tribunals, ombudsmen, etc., that we may be able to express our dissatisfaction to – at the same time, as being content to live within our means, though, admittedly, this may not be successful, or an easy thing to do, as many of us know from experience.

Gift or Wage?

Another point we should pick up from what Paul says to the Philippians is that he describes what they sent as a *gift*, as indeed it was – an unsolicited, genuine expression of their love for, and concern for him.

Paul was not working in or for the church at Philippi when they sent their gift. However, when someone is working as, say an invited speaker for a church or organization, the situation is entirely different. The church has asked this person to commit themselves to do a specific teaching or preaching job for them. Jesus Himself ruled on this matter when He sent out His disciples on a mission. He told them to: '... remain in the same house, eating and drinking what they provide, for the labourer deserves his wages...' (Luke 10:7).

Paul repeats this maxim when instructing Timothy how to act in the church at Ephesus:

> Let the elders who rule well be considered worthy of double honour, especially those who labour in preaching and teaching. For the Scripture says, 'You shall not muzzle an ox when it treads out the grain,' and, 'The labourer deserves his wages.' (1 Tim. 5:17-18)

Neither Jesus nor Paul says that the labourer deserves a *gift*. We do not give a 'gift' to a carpenter for repairing a floor, a builder for constructing a wall, a lawyer (attorney) for writing a will, or a dentist for repairing our teeth. That would be inappropriate language, and using it in the connection with Christian teaching and preaching indicates a serious misunderstanding. I mention this since, in some Christian circles, not limited to any one denomination, it has been common to describe what is given to an invited speaker, teacher, evangelist as a 'gift to cover expenses'.

However, a gift, by definition, is something given that is unearned. It is not intended as a payment for services rendered. When you give someone a gift for their birthday, it is not payment for anything, it is a token to say that they are appreciated and loved. That is, its monetary value is not important (or shouldn't be), but the thought behind it is.

Also, wages are proportionate, or should be, to the work done and to the person doing it. Gifts are not proportionate to anything, and giving a gift rather than wages for work done, although it may sound spiritual, can be the exact opposite, as, it may on occasions be a way of avoiding giving a worker what is their due for the work they have done and thus, in fact, defrauding them. I have known gifted evangelists from various denominational backgrounds who have told me that a church that had invited them to speak sometimes gave them a 'gift' that did not even cover their fare home, and I am not simply talking about the distant past. Related to that is the giving of 'petrol money' as expenses which do not add up to the cost of running the car – which is readily available these days on the internet. That also should not be. There is an almost unbelievable illustration of this on the FIEC website where Trevor Archer relates how a friend of his:

> ...completed a 120-mile round journey by car to speak at a rural church. If the cars in their car park were anything to go by, this was obviously a wealthy congregation. After the service, the treasurer shuffled up to him in time-honoured fashion in the car park with an envelope, which he discreetly slipped into the preacher's Bible, whilst whispering, in best Spooks fashion: "Something for your journey, brother". On his way home my friend stopped for a coffee and opened the envelope. It contained three boiled sweets![1]

It is important to know that 'gifts' given as wages for invited, designated service, are not normally recognized by tax authorities (certainly not by the HMRC in UK, or the IRS in the USA). Although they are sometimes called honoraria,[2] they are, in fact, wages or fees for services rendered, and therefore taxable as income at the usual rates. Therefore, a church or organization should avoid using the word 'gift' for what is the payment of a fee.

Of course, it is a wonderful aspect of Christian love to give gifts to the Lord's servants, who are not working for us or our church or organisation but are, for example, missionaries in another country, or workers for another church or organisation. Such gifts will bring great joy to them as they did to Paul. However, if we invite people to work specifically for us, and they commit themselves to do so, we should also commit ourselves to them and let them know where they stand. Now, how that should be negotiated is up to the people concerned, but it is a symptom of a problem, if inviting parties are highly specific as to what they expect from the person they have invited, but are not at all specific when it comes to their expression of reciprocal commitment. That sometimes results in workers being remunerated at far less than the

---

[1]   See the FIEC article https://fiec.org.uk/resources/gifts-for-visiting-preachers-the-good-the-bad-and-the-ugly

[2]   Technically, an honorarium is a token payment made to bestow recognition to an individual for services they perform, for which payment is not required. Typically, an honorarium is issued when custom or propriety forbids a price to be set. Therefore, payment to the recipient is at the discretion of the payer.

minimum wage for that particular country. The reason why is not hard to guess and sadly leads to a reputation for stinginess and meanness that reflects very poorly on the gospel itself – witness the horror story above.

To sum up: *gifts* are to be given to those believers that are not working at our request, but who we wish to support. Appropriate *wages* should be given by churches and organisations to those believers that they invite to work for them.

As an example of how this worked out in a church in New Testament times, we have Paul's statement in 1 Timothy 5. He is giving instructions to his younger colleague and son in the faith, Timothy, about how things should be done in the church at Ephesus. Timothy is to note carefully which leaders are ruling well, and especially those who work hard at teaching. They are to be counted worthy of *double honour*, that is, they should not only be held in respect for their teaching: they should also be remunerated for it.

It would seem that these particular teaching elders were not initially remunerated for their teaching. That only started after they had proved their capability and commitment. Not surprisingly, there is a back story to the situation into which Paul was writing. In fact, there is more information in the New Testament about the church at Ephesus than there is on any other church. Paul had spent two years teaching there (Acts 19:10) and after he left, on his way to Jerusalem, he called the church elders from Ephesus to meet with him at Miletus, since he had not been able to revisit Ephesus, as he perhaps had hoped. He said a number of things to these leaders, but the one that is relevant here is this:

> And now I commend you to God and to the word of his grace, which is able to build you up and to give you the inheritance among all those who are sanctified. I coveted no one's silver or gold or apparel. You yourselves know that these hands ministered to my necessities and to those who were with me. In all things I have shown you that by working hard in this way we must help the weak and remember the words of the Lord Jesus, how he himself said, 'It is more blessed to give than to receive.' (Acts 20:32-35)

This whole farewell speech is very moving. Paul is careful to avoid any accusation of covetousness as he reminds the leaders that they experienced him as a person who worked manually in order to finance himself, and his team that was with him. He now tells them that this was to encourage them to do the same. Remember, Paul is here speaking to the *leaders*, those who hold the first line of responsibility for teaching, preaching and pastoring in the church. He clearly expects them to be people that have a job for which they are remunerated.

Paul's exhortation is based on his own example:

> For you remember, brothers, our labour and toil: we worked night and day, that we might not be a burden to any of you, while we proclaimed to you the gospel of God. You are witnesses, and God also, how holy and righteous and blameless was our conduct towards you believers. For you know how, like a father with his children, we exhorted each one of you and encouraged you and charged you to walk in a manner worthy of God, who calls you into his own kingdom and glory. (1 Thess. 2:9-12)

Tim Chester writes: 'Presumably this involved Paul making tents by day and teaching the gospel in the evening. It is perhaps a model more church leaders should follow. We assume freedom from secular work is the ideal for ministers, but Paul didn't. It was important for him to set an example to new Christians of earning one's way.'

Some years after having instructed the leaders in the church at Ephesus to work with their own hands, he writes to them again through Timothy, and modifies this instruction when he introduces the idea of *double honour*. The church membership and leadership were not to stand idly by, and watch people exhaust themselves in ministry, especially teaching, in addition to their ordinary work. The church must be prepared to relieve the pressure in part, or whole, by paying wages to those that have earned the right to such support by the quality of their teaching, and their commitment to it.

The New Testament, therefore, presents us with an interestingly complex situation. Paul had the right to support but he did not always use it, and carried on with his professional tent-making. He did not give in to the secular-sacred divide (SSD). He tells church leaders to use him as a model, and likewise to work at a remunerative job as well as teaching the church, with the proviso that if doing both proves increasingly stressful, and (not, or) if their teaching is good, the church should remunerate them, to lift the pressure. This created a healthy tension: the leaders did not expect to be paid, and the church was not allowed to think that they should not be paid.

That model has obvious strengths since it resists the simplistic, and unbiblical, SSD of the sort: 'That's the pastor's job, he's paid for it; it's not mine, I'm paid to be an accountant.' The net result is that many churches have members who are gifted people who, because they are not officially 'ordained', are not able (or permitted) to exercise their God-given gifts publicly; and this can lead, as I have often observed, to frustration, and sometimes to them leaving that church for somewhere else where their gifts can be employed.

Having said that, there are many churches and organisations that do recognise this problem, and so encourage their gifted members to get involved in public ministry; and there are also excellent short-term courses that help train people for precisely this kind of activity. However, some church leaders complain to me that people that they judge to have real potential may respond to any suggestion in that direction by saying: 'That's what you are paid for, I'm not.' The SSD again!

Of course, one reason for this reaction is the widespread, unbiblical concept of 'full-time Christian work' that we discussed earlier.

In order to break this log-jam we need to get across to Christian believers, that it is possible, even desirable, to have a job or career, and *simultaneously* to be a teacher, evangelist, pastor, youth leader, etc., in the church. It stands to reason, also, that if we are going to reach people in 'ordinary' jobs and we have no idea of what it means to do such a job, our credibility with such people is likely to be very low or non-existent.

If you will permit a personal reference, I have tried to do this all my life. When I was much younger, I saw it modelled in a friend and mentor, also a university teacher. I learned by his example that it was possible to have a career and, in his and my cases, be both an academic, a speaker on the intellectual defence of Christianity, a Bible teacher and Christian author. I also saw that it would involve a great deal of time investment. I could never have done it if my wife, Sally, and my children had not been prepared to give me the space necessary for me to get into Scripture and develop whatever abilities I had. They often set me free, for example, to go for a week to Hungary where I would do mathematics all day long, and then do several hours of Bible teaching in the evenings.

I am also aware that in our contemporary world, particularly in the West, life is increasingly pressurized. Nevertheless, I am still convinced that it is worth the attempt to get back to a semblance of what used to be fairly common practice. It is one way in which we can combat the insidious inroads of secular thinking in the church.

I would strongly encourage people who are in employment, not to assume that their employment is not a ministry, nor to think that they cannot have a valuable ministry that can run parallel to their employment, and, like that employment, be done for the Lord, and with His help. You should not assume that you cannot be a Bible teacher, preacher, counsellor, etc. simply because God has called you to work in a factory or shop, or you are engaged in one of the professions. You should rather seek God's guidance to discover the gifts He has given you, and to find a sphere in which you can develop those abilities so that they are not lost to those who could benefit from them.

Paul and Christian Charity

There is one further aspect of Paul's attitude to the material support of Christian work, that is needed to balance the picture. We have seen that he did not ask for such support for himself, but he did not hesitate to ask it for others that he saw in need. In fact, he makes a very strong appeal to the church at Corinth, covering two entire chapters (2 Cor. 8, 9), that they should make a regular collection, not for Paul, but for the Lord's work in general, and for the relief of poorer believers in Jerusalem, in particular. The importance of this charitable collection is to be seen in the fact that Paul himself, in collaboration with some local churches, was forming a strong team of people of known moral integrity to take the money for the relief of believers in Jerusalem. He reminds them that the churches of Macedonia, who were poor compared with Corinth, had already contributed more than generously to the cause, and so, on a principle of fairness, the Corinthians ought to be prepared to do the same.

He lays down the fundamental principle of proportional giving in a lovely passage that points us to the paradoxically enriching voluntary poverty of the Lord Jesus in His incarnation:

> For you know the grace of our Lord Jesus Christ, that though he was rich, yet for your sake he became poor, so that you by his poverty might become rich. And in this matter I give my judgement: this benefits you, who a year ago started not only to do this work but also to desire to do it. So now finish doing it as well, so that your readiness in desiring it may be matched by your completing it out of what you have. For if the readiness is there, it is acceptable according to what a person has, not according to what he does not have. For I do not mean that others should be eased and you burdened, but that as a matter of fairness your abundance at the present time should supply their need, so that their abundance may supply your need, that there may be fairness. As it is written, 'Whoever gathered much had nothing left over, and whoever gathered little had no lack.' (2 Cor. 8:9-15)

Paul later adds:

> Each one must give as he has decided in his heart, not reluctantly or under compulsion, for God loves a cheerful giver. And God is able to make all grace abound to you, so that having all sufficiency in all things at all times, you may abound in every good work. As it is written, 'He has distributed freely, he has given to the poor; his righteousness endures for ever.' (2 Cor. 9:7-9)

Corinth was a wealthy city, and Paul shows himself well aware of the ins and outs of economic activity in the way that he heads off the kind of response that would have written him off as a dreamer, who knew little of the complexities of the world of finance.

Paul gives an illustration from the familiar world of agricultural economics:

> The point is this: whoever sows sparingly will also reap sparingly, and whoever sows bountifully will also reap bountifully. Each one must give as he has decided in his heart, not reluctantly or under compulsion, for God loves a cheerful giver. And God is able to make all grace abound to you, so that having all sufficiency in all things at all times, you may abound in every good work. As it is written: 'He has distributed freely, he has given to the poor; his righteousness endures forever.'

> He who supplies seed to the sower and bread for food will supply and multiply your seed for sowing and increase the harvest of your righteousness. You will be enriched in every way to be generous in every way, which through us will produce thanksgiving to God. For the ministry of this service is not only supplying the needs of the saints but is also overflowing in many thanksgivings to God. By their approval of this service, they will glorify God because of your submission flowing from your confession of the gospel of Christ, and the generosity of your contribution for them and for all others, while they long for you and pray for you, because of the surpassing grace of God upon you. Thanks be to God for his inexpressible gift!' (2 Cor. 9:6-15)

His first point is obvious, at least, it would be to any farmer. If you do not sow (enough) you will not reap (enough). However, the idea that giving to the Lord's work, for instance, the relief of other Christians, is to be regarded as *sowing,* may not have occurred to everyone. For a farmer sows in the hope of reaping, but this giving was to poor believers who could not respond in kind. But they could respond in another important way. The harvest that Paul envisages is a harvest of righteousness and thanksgiving to God. It is a moral and spiritual harvest, both for giver and recipient, and God is glorified in the process. The by-products of work have been used to reach the goal.

Paul has another point to make that would not have been lost on the city workers in Corinth: 'He who supplies seed to the sower and bread for food will supply and multiply your seed for sowing and increase the harvest of your righteousness. You will be enriched in every way to be generous in every way, which through us will produce thanksgiving to God' (2 Cor. 9:10-11).

Paul understands, that for a farmer, seed represents both income and capital. If all the seed that is harvested one year is sold then there will be no seed to sow for the following year, and the farmer will go bankrupt and leave destitute himself, his family, and those who work for him. The problem, for any farmer, and any system that involves both capital and labour, is: how to divide the harvest – how much do you store for sowing, how much do you sell and, when you sell it, how do you divide it up between your needs, wages for your farmhands, and what do you give to the Lord's work? Each person must work that out for themselves.

That is never easy. I used to think that I would be able to solve this kind of problem – dividing up my time, my money, my energies – by the time I was thirty, and then I would begin to live. A wise mentor told me that I had it all wrong – solving this kind of problem was living. I have found that change in perspective very helpful as it takes a lot of the pressure, indeed, irritation out of challenging decisions, even if it doesn't necessarily make them much easier.

As to the proportion one should give, in the Old Testament a tithe was prescribed for Israel – that was used in part to maintain the Levites, whose responsibility was the tabernacle and the service of God.

In the New Testament, the fundamental principle that Paul laid down is:

> Each one must give as he has decided in his heart, not reluctantly or under compulsion, for God loves a cheerful giver. And God is able to make all grace abound to you, so that having all sufficiency in all things at all times, you may abound in every good work. As it is written, 'He has distributed freely, he has given to the poor; his righteousness endures forever. (2 Cor. 9:7-9)

Questions

1. What are the basic biblical principles of supporting the work of the gospel? What part do/should you play in this?
2. What do you think of the idea of having a career or job and at the same time being involved in Bible teaching and evangelism? Are there dangers? Advantages? Discuss them.
3. In your view, what are the most important principles of Christian giving?
4. How do you work out a sense of proportion in your giving?

APPENDIX B

INSIGHTS FROM NEUROSCIENCE

In Chapter 1 we saw the importance of the work-rest cycle in connection with the Sabbath that provided a God dimension by flagging up the importance of seeing our work in the context both of creation, and the narrative of redemption. That gives us a framework, or big picture, in which to fit the detail of our work and give it an ultimate meaning beyond itself – in other words, a world-view significance.

However, realism tells us that many people, including some of our colleagues and workmates, do not have any larger framework for their work and lives. Indeed, I am sure that most of my readers will be aware that, contributing to the the dominant atheism of our western culture, some powerful voices dogmatically deny that ultimate meaning exists. One of them was the late Steven Weinberg, a Nobel laureate for physics who said: 'The more the universe seems comprehensible, the more it also seems pointless.'[1]

Owen Barfield, British philosopher, poet, critic and one of the Inklings group of intellectuals that surrounded C.S. Lewis, pointed out a strange paradox:

---

[1]   *The First Three Minutes*, (London: Fontana, 1983), 149.

Amid all the menacing signs that surround us in the middle of this twentieth century, perhaps the one that fills thoughtful people with the greatest foreboding is the growing general sense of meaninglessness. It is this which underlies most of the other threats. How is it that the more able man becomes to manipulate the world to his advantage, the less he can perceive any meaning in it?[2]

'Manipulating the world' is one way of describing much of the work that humans do, and therefore Barfield's question is important in the context of work.

Failure to perceive any meaning has clearly got to do with the way in which we pay attention to the world. As I said in Chapter 2, how we pay attention to the world is the subject of neuroscientist Iain McGilchrist's book, *The Matter with Things: Our Brains, Our Delusions and the Unmaking of the World.*[3]

Let me remind you that his research relates to the fact that the human brain is composed of two hemispheres that, although they are both involved in virtually all brain activity, there are nevertheless important differences between them.[4]

He argues that there is an asymmetry between the two hemispheres with the left emphasising apprehension, and the right comprehension, so that each of them pays attention to the world in a different way, and therefore gives rise to a different kind of knowledge, as illustrated in the following table:

The left hemisphere	*The right hemisphere*
manipulates/controls	understands/trusts
categorises by features	categorises by gestalt
knows things as objects	knows people as subjects
mechanism	organism
simple rhythm	music
isolated incidents	story
theory, the map	experience, the terrain
science, technology	the arts, philosophy, religion

---

[2]   *The Rediscovery of Meaning*, (Oxford: Barfield Press, 2013) p.11.

[3]   London, Perspectiva Press, 2021.

[4]   A helpful presentation of his views is to be found at https://www.youtube.com/watch?v=U99dQrZdVTg

Applying these ideas to the development of culture, McGilchrist argues that historically the West has over-emphasised the left hemisphere to the neglect of the right. He writes: 'We have become dominated by our left hemispheres that have mesmerized us to think that their mechanistic, reductionist, manipulative approach gives us the whole picture of reality, whereas we have become blind to the integrative, holistic, and more intelligent meaning-yielding perspective of the right hemisphere.'

The very interesting conclusion that McGilchrist draws from his work is that the historical development of the dominance of the reductionist world-view, and its opposition to meaning and giving explanations, can be explained by the fact that there is a battle between the hemispheres – a battle, that is, only from the perspective of the left hemisphere that cannot be aware of what the right hemisphere knows, and thinks it knows it all and so can go it alone, although it is actually more dependent on the right hemisphere, than the right is on it.

We cited in Chapter 2 what happens when the left hemisphere goes it alone: 'The tendency of the left hemisphere is to narrow focus so drastically that it fails to see the broad picture at all, and therefore cannot detect that anything is missing when its impoverished picture becomes a supposed representation of the whole.'

This is surely a convincing answer to Barfield's paradox, in that it shows that the more able human beings have become to manipulate the world to their advantage, the less they can perceive any meaning in it, because they have concentrated so much on left hemisphere analysis, that they have reached the (logically incoherent[5]) conclusion that the natural sciences tell us everything. They might not like it, but their view that reduces the universe into a mass of things – and atoms are things – is literally a half-brained view of reality.

The late Lord Jonathan Sacks, former Chief Rabbi of the UK and Commonwealth, summarised McGilchrist's work very neatly: 'Science takes things apart to see how they work.

---

[5] See my *Can Science Explain Everything?* (London: The Good Book Company), 2019.

Religion puts things together to see what they mean. Without going into neuro-scientific detail, the first is a predominantly left-brain activity, the second is associated with the right hemisphere.'

This means, in general, that we are faced with the fact that the way we pay attention to the world affects our understanding of reality, and our value system. We cannot completely escape the influence of the culture in which we live, but neuroscience can help us be aware of tendencies to look for, both in ourselves and others, so that we can recognise what is going on, and react accordingly. If we let our left hemisphere dominate, we shall think that things matter more than people, and if we let the right dominate, as we should, people will matter more than things.

Oliver Schultheiss, a psychologist and neuroscientist from the University of Erlangen-Nuremberg, lists certain traits that characterise left-brain thinking:

> Individuals who get stuck in a left hemisphere information processing mode ... have a peculiar maladaptive mindset ... characterized ... by reality distortion through denial of expectation-violating information, an inability to deal with ambiguity, a tendency to treat others as mere tools for the advancement of one's interests and goals, and a profound lack of empathy.

We need to be aware of these character traits since many, if not most, of us will have to deal with people like this in our work environment. For instance, Jeff the electrician's boss was left hemisphere dominated. He was only interested in the number of electrical 'things' installed in a given period of time, whereas Jeff as a person with values, did not matter to him at all. However, Jeff was using both parts of his brain – the left to do the detailed underfloor wiring, and the right to check the ethical quality of his work, in light of his big-picture awareness that the Lord was watching him. Jeff let the right hemisphere dominate.

Furthermore, we may even find some of the tendencies, listed by Schultheiss, within ourselves, that we shall have to fight to overcome, if we are going to mature as Christian believers, in the workplace and elsewhere.

McGilchrist's title, *The Matter with Things*, speaks volumes when taken in conjunction with Jesus' teaching: 'Seek first the kingdom of God and all these things will be added onto you.' The left hemisphere is mesmerised with things. It tells us to make them the chief goal in life for our work, whereas Jesus instructs us to allow the right hemisphere to dominate our thinking, the hemisphere that is aware of him and his kingdom. The fact that the left brain *cannot* appreciate what the right is seeing, needs to be taken seriously as we try to evaluate what is happening to us when the kingdom of God seems to dim and fade in light of our preoccupation with things. Yes, there is something very much *the matter with things*.

When Jesus asked Peter to let down his nets, Peter's left hemisphere took note of the facts surrounding the failed night's fishing. His right hemisphere took note of Jesus' command: he let it dominate and obeyed.

We should note that McGilchrist rejects the widespread but false idea that we are nothing but our brains. He emphatically states: 'You are *not* your brain, you are a living human being …'[6] From a Christian perspective I must point out that there is a difficulty with McGilchrist's analysis. His left-brain dominant view leads him to be very suspicious of defined doctrine of the sort that characterises a robust Christian faith. In fact, although he speaks of God, it is not the God and Father of our Lord Jesus Christ. McGilchrist says he favours pantheism – all in God and God in all – which is sometimes not only difficult to define but also hard to differentiate from full-blown pantheism. I quote him in the spirit of Paul at Athens who cited pagan sources as having correct insights ("In him we live and move and have our being" and "We are also his offspring") even though he makes clear that their concept of God is completely inadequate and they need to repent and trust in the only true God, who has revealed himself in the person of Jesus Christ whom he has designated as the final judge, by raising him from the dead as a fact of history.

---

6   *The Matter with Things*, p.47. The reader wishing more on this topic could refer to brain scientist Sharon Dirckx' book: *Am I just my Brain*, (London, The Good News Company, 2019).

BIBLIOGRAPHY

Tim Chester, *The Busy Christians Guide to Busyness*, Leicester, IVP, 2006.

Ken Costa, *God at Work*, Nashville, W. Publishing Group, 2016.

Mark Greene, *The Great Divide*, London, LICC, 2013.

Os Guinness, *The Call*, Nashville, Zondervan, 1998.

Iain McGilchrist, *The Master and His Emissary*, Yale, University Press, 2009.

Iain McGilchrist, *The Matter with Things*, London, Perspectiva, 2021.

Marcus Nodder, *City Lives*, Leyland UK, 10 Publishing, 2018.

John Rinehart, *Gospel Patrons*, Reclaimed Publishing, 2013

Dorothy Sayers, *Why Work?* in *Letters to a Diminished Church*, Nashville, W. Publishing Group, 2004.

The Theology of Work Project, https://www.theologyofwork.org. There is a great deal of resource material here that is worth consulting on specific work-related issues.

also available from Christian Focus Publications...

... warm, witty, wise, biblical, personal and kind.
– Mark Greene

PROVING GROUND

40 REFLECTIONS ON GROWING FAITH AT WORK

GRAHAM HOOPER

ISBN: 978-1-5271-0845-5

Proving Ground

40 Reflections on Growing Faith at Work

Graham Hooper

An honest and realistic look at why how we work matters.

There is no such thing as untested Christian faith.

The Bible shows us how testing experiences are common to every Christian and are part of God's good work in making us the people he wants us to be. As we spend so much of our time working, (whether in the home, in voluntary work, study or in a paid job), our work, like every part of our life, provides opportunities to prove for ourselves that God is real and at work in his world for good.

Graham Hooper has written this challenging and encouraging book for all Christians, but particularly for those struggling to 'live out' their faith at work, or questioning the worth of what they are doing.

Graham writes with the conviction that the Bible's teaching about work is inclusive, covering every type of work at every stage of life; that the Bible is a message of good news with a universal application; and that it is also honest and realistic about the pressures of daily work and the way these often test our faith in a just and loving God.

It's this truly biblical view of work, grounded in Graham's own experience, which he presents in this book.

Christian Focus Publications

Our mission statement –

STAYING FAITHFUL

In dependence upon God we seek to impact the world through literature faithful to His infallible Word, the Bible. Our aim is to ensure that the Lord Jesus Christ is presented as the only hope to obtain forgiveness of sin, live a useful life and look forward to heaven with Him.

Our books are published in four imprints:

CHRISTIAN
FOCUS

Popular works including biographies, commentaries, basic doctrine and Christian living.

CHRISTIAN
HERITAGE

Books representing some of the best material from the rich heritage of the church.

MENTOR

Books written at a level suitable for Bible College and seminary students, pastors, and other serious readers. The imprint includes commentaries, doctrinal studies, examination of current issues and church history.

CF4•K

Children's books for quality Bible teaching and for all age groups: Sunday school curriculum, puzzle and activity books; personal and family devotional titles, biographies and inspirational stories – because you are never too young to know Jesus!

Christian Focus Publications Ltd,
Geanies House, Fearn, Ross-shire,
IV20 1TW, Scotland, United Kingdom.
www.christianfocus.com